INSPIRATION

David R. Law

New Century Theology

D1197061

Continuum
London and New York

Continuum
The Tower Building, 11 York Road, London SE1 7NX
370 Lexington Avenue, New York NY 10017–6503

www.continuumbooks.com

© David R. Law 2001

All rights reserved. No part of this publication may be reproduced or transmitted in any form or by any means, electronic or mechanical, including photocopying, recording or any information storage or retrieval system, without prior permission in writing from the publishers.

First published 2001

British Library Cataloguing-in-Publication Data
A catalogue record for this book is available from the British Library.

ISBN 0–8264–5183–7

Designed and typeset by YHT Ltd, London.
Printed and bound in Great Britain
by Biddles Ltd, *www.biddles.co.uk*

Contents

Preface

This book is the result of my growing conviction over the past few years that biblical scholars – with some notable exceptions – have paid insufficient attention to the question of the inspiration of the Bible. My own encounter with the Bible has convinced me that this collection of ancient texts contains a power to transform the lives of human beings and open up new possibilities for human existence. The following study is an attempt to articulate the nature of this encounter and provide a framework within which it can again become meaningful to speak of the inspiration of scripture.

No academic work – particularly in such a discipline as theology – is ever written in isolation, but owes much to friends, family and institutions. This book is no exception and has benefited from support and encouragement from a variety of sources. The award of a fellowship by the Alexander von Humboldt Foundation enabled me to pursue research on the question of biblical inspiration at the Evangelisch-Theologische Fakultät at the Christian-Albrechts-Universität Kiel, and to bring this work to completion. I am grateful both to the generosity of the Foundation and to Professor Dr Johannes Schilling of the University of Kiel for making my stay in Germany so agreeable and productive. It was Professor Dr Christoph Schwöbel, however, now of Heidelberg University, who invited me to

Kiel, for which I am grateful. I am indebted also to the University of Manchester for giving me the study leave that made it possible to take up the Humboldt Fellowship and complete this book.

It would be out of keeping with the theme of this study not to acknowledge the 'inspiration' that I have received from family and friends. The critical and thought-provoking comments of my Manchester colleagues Professor David A. Pailin and Dr Todd Klutz have helped me to address – at least to my own satisfaction – the weaknesses of my defence of biblical inspiration. Needless to say, any weaknesses that have nevertheless found their way into the book remain my responsibility. The hospitality of Paul and Ursula Gesk provided me with the space to get on with my work and played an important role in making my stay in Germany such a pleasant one. I would also like to thank my son Alexander for his forbearance and patience during his father's absence in Germany. Last, but certainly not least, I would like to acknowledge the support, encouragement and inspiration of my wife Claudia, to whom this book is dedicated.

David R. Law
Tarp
July 2000

Für meine geliebte Frau
Claudia

1

The problem of biblical authority

Why is the Bible important and, if it is important, on what principles is this importance based? These are significant questions, for, as Paul J. Achtemeier points out,

> Unless [the] Bible can in some way claim a unique status and authority in its content and intention, the Christian faith becomes what its opponents, past and present, claim it is: a human attempt to solve human problems, suffering from the delusion that it represents something more.[1]

For apologetic reasons, then, it is important that theologians strive to articulate the nature of biblical authority as well as providing grounds for our acceptance of this authority. We may not be able to compel non-Christians to accept the claims made for the Bible but it is arguably one of the apologetic tasks of the Christian theologian to articulate the grounds for accepting the Bible as authoritative.

It has, furthermore, traditionally been claimed that the Bible is not merely a collection of ancient texts, but that these texts speak, or have at least the potential to speak, to

[1] Paul J. Achtemeier, *The Inspiration of Scripture* (Philadelphia: Westminster Press, 1980), p. 13.

human beings today. These texts, it is said, are not merely of historical interest for understanding the beliefs and practices of long-past epochs of human history. Despite their distance from us in time, place and culture, these texts, it is claimed, address us here and now. 'Christianity', as Gore puts it, 'professes to be not a mere record of the past, but a present life, and there is no life where there is no experience.'[2] Christians believe that the Bible plays an important role in the evocation and sustenance of this life. But how is this collection of ancient texts able to achieve this? How can the Bible evoke and sustain 'a present life' on the part of those who commit themselves to it?

There is, however, another important reason for attempting to construct a theology of inspiration. In recent years a number of biblical scholars have become increasingly concerned at the non-theological or even anti-theological nature of much modern biblical scholarship. Francis Watson comments that 'Modern biblical scholarship has devised a variety of strategies for concealing, evading or denying the simple fact that Christian faith has its own *distinctive* reasons for concern with the Bible.'[3] The consequence of this, as Stephen Fowl points out, is that 'the discipline of biblical theology, in its most common form, is systematically unable to generate serious theological interpretation of scripture'.[4] A similar point is made by

[2] Charles Gore, 'The Holy Spirit and inspiration', in Charles Gore (ed.), *Lux Mundi: A Series of Studies in the Religion of the Incarnation* (London: John Murray, 1890), pp. 313–62; 315.

[3] Francis Watson, *Text and Truth* (Edinburgh: T&T Clark, 1997), p. viii (original emphasis). Watson is, however, overstating his case. It is more accurate to speak not of biblical scholars concealing or denying that the Christian faith has its own distinctive reasons for concern with the Bible, but of their interest in the Bible being motivated by concerns that are frequently not distinctively Christian. This constitutes an evasion rather than a concealment or denial of the Christian nature of the Bible.

[4] Stephen E. Fowl, *Engaging Scripture* (Oxford: Blackwell, 1998), p. 1.

Werner Jeanrond when he speaks of the necessity of a 'theological perspective' in order to release the 'semantic potential' of the biblical texts.[5] Watson, Fowl and Jeanrond have all been concerned to recover such a theological perspective and thereby provide the basis for a theological interpretation of scripture. In this study I wish to take the argument back a stage further and ask the question: What are the grounds for attempting a theological interpretation of the Bible? What is it about this book, or rather collection of books, that makes theological interpretation an appropriate, indeed perhaps *the* appropriate method for interpreting it? It is my contention that these questions are best addressed by means of a theology of inspiration.

Our first task, however, is to examine the cause of the problem, namely the crisis in biblical authority. Why has the Bible lost authority?

The crisis of biblical authority

The authority of the Bible has been increasingly undermined in the last 250 years.[6] In contrast to earlier ages, the authority of the Bible is no longer taken for granted and many, perhaps indeed the majority of people in the West no longer accept the Bible as authoritative. There are several reasons for this crisis of biblical authority.

[5] Werner Jeanrond, 'After hermeneutics: The relationship between theology and biblical studies', in Francis Watson (ed.), *The Open Text* (London: SCM Press, 1993), pp. 85–102; 88.

[6] For an account of the factors which have led to the crisis of biblical authority, see J. K. S. Reid, *The Authority of Scripture: A Study of the Reformation and Post-Reformation Understanding of the Bible* (London: Methuen, 1957), ch. 1; Henning Graf Reventlow, *The Authority of the Bible and the Rise of the Modern World*, trans. John Bowden (London: SCM Press, 1984).

The modern emphasis on autonomy

The Bible's status and role in society have been affected by the general questioning of the concept of authority that has been taking place since the Enlightenment. According to Kant, in *What is Enlightenment?*, the enlightened human being does not follow blindly the dictates of others but the guidance of his or her own autonomously exercised reason.[7] This emphasis on autonomy and the concomitant suspicion of authority have intensified since the 1960s, and it is no exaggeration to say that the crisis of authority has spread to every area of life. Furthermore, the principle has come to be accepted that any institution or individual claiming authority must *justify* that claim. The Bible is not exempt from this general critique and suspicion of authority. Like any other authority, the Bible must provide justification for its claim to authority if this claim is to be acknowledged.

Suspicion of the past

The suspicion of authority that has arisen since the Enlightenment has frequently been accompanied by suspicion of the past. Lash sums up the problem well:

> Perhaps one of the features that most sharply distinguishes 'modern' from 'classical' culture is that the mere fact that something has been said or done in the past no longer supplies it with authoritative status. Indeed the opposite may well be the case. In so far as the only ground on which a 'voice' claims to speak to us authoritatively is that it speaks to us from the past, we are likely to experience it, not as the

[7] Immanuel Kant, 'An answer to the question: "What is Enlightenment?"', in *Kant: Political Writings*, trans. H. B. Nisbet, ed. Hans Reiss (Cambridge: Cambridge University Press, 1991), pp. 54–60.

> liberating voice of truth, but as oppressive, restrictive, cramping our style.[8]

There is also the problem of why the solutions of the past should be applicable to the very different cultural milieu of the present. As Lash puts it,

> Our problem is that the past no longer speaks to us authoritatively, with authority, partly because we are very conscious of how different the past is from the present and, being conscious of this, we are no longer confident that the solutions which men applied, in very different contexts, to the problems which confronted them, are necessarily of any great assistance to us as we seek to come to grips with the problems of the present day.[9]

We have become increasingly conscious of the differences between our age and the period in which the biblical texts were composed. Quite simply, we think in fundamentally different categories from the biblical writers. We live in a heliocentric, they in a geocentric universe. They lived in a world populated by supernatural powers, a world in which God was, on occasions, prepared to intervene directly. In contrast, today we tend to look for natural, scientifically explicable causes and do not conceive of the universe as, to borrow the title of Carl Sagan's book, 'a demon-haunted world'.[10] As Pannenberg points out,

> Once it has become conscious of the depth of this gulf,

[8] Nicholas Lash, *Voices of Authority* (London: Sheed and Ward, 1976), p. 59.

[9] Lash, *Voices of Authority*, pp. 61–2.

[10] Carl Sagan, *The Demon-Haunted World: Science as a Candle in the Dark* (London: Headline, 1997).

> no theology can understand itself any longer as 'biblical' in the naive sense, as if it could be materially identical with the conceptions of Paul and John. For in a changed situation the traditional phrases, even when recited literally, do not mean what they did at the time of their original formulation.[11]

It is not only these major cultural differences that place a barrier between ourselves and the biblical texts, however. We have also come to adopt a fundamentally different attitude towards our *own* culture. Lonergan points out that modern culture differs significantly in its self-understanding from classical culture.[12] Classical culture saw itself as definitive and normative. It regarded itself as the only valid culture and all those outside it as barbarians. This view of culture as normative is one that has declined in the modern world, however. We no longer see cultures as unchangeable, eternally valid and normative for future generations. On the contrary, we have become aware of the plurality of cultures, of their historical conditioning, and of how cultures develop and change. This raises two problems concerning the claims to authority made on behalf of ancient texts such as the Bible.

First, claims that the writings of a particular culture are authoritative would seem to be based on a failure to perceive the historical conditioning of that culture. From this perspective, the attempt to set up a particular culture as definitive and normative for the present constitutes an attempt to make a particular section of a dynamic process

[11] Wolfhart Pannenberg, 'The crisis of the scripture principle', in *Basic Questions in Theology*, trans. George H. Kehm, 3 vols (London: SCM Press, 1970–73), vol. 1, pp. 1–14; 8–9.

[12] Bernard J. F. Lonergan, *A Second Collection*, ed. William F. J. Ryan and Bernard J. Tyrell (London: Darton, Longman & Todd, 1974), pp. 92–3, 206.

of development determinative of the later stages of that development. To insist on the authority of the texts of an ancient culture would thus seem to be a misunderstanding of the dynamic nature of cultural development and indicates a failure to think historically.

Secondly, the culture or cultures which brought into existence allegedly 'authoritative' texts may be so different from our own that we must question the appropriateness of allowing these texts to determine our thinking and acting in the present. To attempt to transpose classical culture on to the present, as if the situations of ancient and modern culture were identical or at least highly compatible, may again seem to be a failure to think historically. In addition to this, there is the problem that modern culture is not a homogeneous entity but is itself pluralist in nature, raising the question of how the insights of the Bible are to be applied in such a pluralist world. As Lash points out,

> we must not lose sight of the fact that the 'world' in which we live today is not one world, but several. Today the gospel has to be 'heard' and responded to, articulated, expressed and obeyed, in a wide variety of radically different social, cultural, linguistic and philosophical contexts.[13]

The rise of historical scholarship

A further reason for the crisis of biblical authority is that academic theology for the most part pays little attention to questions of authority. Abraham notes that the widespread silence of theologians on the subject of biblical authority is

[13] Lash, *Voices of Authority*, pp. 34–5.

an implicit admission that modern theology has little use for the concept.[14] This is the result of a fundamental shift since the Enlightenment in the way the Bible has been treated. The application of historical-critical approaches to the Bible and the uncovering of the different stages in which the Bible came into existence, and the discovery of internal inconsistencies, contradictions and sometimes downright errors in the Bible, have led – in academic theology at least – to the abandonment of the oracular conception of the Bible. The Bible is no longer understood as an infallible and authoritative compendium of divine truths, but as a work that all too clearly bears the marks of fallible human involvement. One of the theological consequences of this has been that the Bible is – outside fundamentalist circles – no longer treated *deductively*. This point is well made by Lonergan, who writes: 'Theology was a deductive, and it has become largely an empirical science . . . Where before the step from premisses to conclusions was brief, simple, and certain, today the steps from data to interpretation are long, arduous, and, at best, probable.'[15]

Moreover, concepts of biblical authority play no significant role in the way the modern biblical scholar carries out his or her investigations of the Bible. Rahner comments that 'the average Catholic exegete, while not denying or questioning the inspiration of the Bible, simply leaves it aside in his exegetical work; he seems unable to make it relevant to his own labors'.[16] Although the biblical scholar may well be motivated by respect, perhaps even reverence, for the biblical texts, the conviction that the Bible is divinely inspired and therefore authoritative does not

[14] William Abraham, *The Divine Inspiration of Holy Scripture* (Oxford: OUP, 1981), pp. 6, 48.

[15] Lonergan, *Second Collection*, pp. 58–9.

[16] Karl Rahner, *Inspiration in the Bible* (New York: Herder and Herder, 1961), p. 7.

determine the tools of biblical criticism. Outside fundamentalist circles, authority plays little or no role in the doing of academic theology and is certainly not employed as a hermeneutical tool for eliciting the meaning of the biblical texts.

Interdenominational developments

The structures of authority within which theology has traditionally been done have been increasingly dismantled. As Barr points out, in previous ages theology took place in a clearly demarcated framework of authority provided by the theologian's denomination. It was this framework of authority that allowed theologians and church leaders to speak of the Bible in terms of authority. Barr writes:

> Within the older authority structures the authority of the Bible occupied a high place in the hierarchy: theoretically at least it was one of the very highest courts of appeal for all sorts of authority, and it therefore had a defined place, very high in the hierarchical order. It was scarcely doubted that the appeal to scripture formed a major ground for discriminating between theologies, for preferring one and rejecting another.[17]

The framework within which it made sense to speak of the authority of the Bible no longer exists, however. According to Barr, 'The setting of theology is now ecumenical and its connection with denominational legal structures has disappeared, apart from minor survivals; there are no longer denominational theologies, and the

[17] James Barr, *The Bible in the Modern World* (London: SCM Press, 1973), p. 29.

means of enforcing them have faded out of existence.'[18] Theology has become pluralistic and the old authority structures that provided a place and role for the concept of biblical authority have been dismantled. The consequence of this is that the Bible can no longer function as the means by which the validity of theologies is judged. In Barr's opinion, 'Within this newer context the idea of the "authority" of the Bible has become anachronistic.'[19]

The problem of biblical plurality

Another threat to claims that the Bible is authoritative is what we might term the problem of biblical plurality. The very diversity of the Bible raises questions of whether it is possible to speak of *the* authority of the Bible. The Bible contains not one, single, homogeneous theology but is made up of a variety of *theologies*, some of which seem to be in competition with each other. Thus Paul's understanding of the law, for example, does not seem to be easily reconcilable with that of the Gospel of Matthew. This raises the question of which of the various theologies of the Bible is most authoritative. On which of the various theological positions present in the Bible is biblical authority grounded?

[18] Ibid., pp. 28–9.

[19] Ibid., p. 29. It is questionable, however, if the authority structures have disintegrated to the degree claimed by Barr. Denominational theologies and theologians continue to exist, as can be seen in chairs of theology associated with particular denominations. This is particularly the case in Germany, where there exist Protestant and Catholic faculties of theology in the universities.

The inappropriateness of the concept of authority to the Bible

The term *authority* (ἐξουσια) is only occasionally present in the Bible, and even then it is applied not to the biblical writings as such but to individuals, above all to Jesus.[20] On these grounds it is argued by some that the concept of authority is inappropriate to the Bible. Goldingay comments,

> Scripture's failure to use terms such as 'authority', 'revelation', and 'canon' in connection with scripture, despite its familiarity with them in other connections, alerts us to the question whether they imply categories that do not correspond well to scripture's nature and function – whether these key technical terms fail to emerge for this purpose in scripture itself because they impose alien categories on scripture; whether the *formal* gap between the way scripture speaks of itself and the way theology has traditionally spoken of scripture is an outward sign of a *real* gap between the two.[21]

Clines questions the appropriateness of applying the concept of authority to the Bible on rather different grounds. He suggests that 'the very concept of "authority" come[s] from a world we have (thankfully) left behind',[22] and finds it strange that feminist writers on authority

[20] Mk 1.22/Mt 7.29/Lk 4.32; Mk 1.27/Lk 4.36; Mk 11.27–33/Mt 21.23–27/Lk 20.1–8; Jn 5.27. See also Mk 6.7/Mt 14.8/Lk 9.1; 2 Cor 10.8; Mt 8.5–13/Lk 7.1–10; Lk 19.17; Acts 9.14; 26.10, 12.

[21] John Goldingay, *Models for Scripture* (Grand Rapids, MI: Eerdmans, 1994), p. 5 (original emphasis).

[22] David J. A. Clines, *What Does Eve Do to Help? and Other Readerly Questions to the Old Testament*; Journal for the Study of the Old Testament Supplement Series 94 (Sheffield: Sheffield Academic Press, 1990), p. 47.

> have not yet seen that 'authority' is a concept from the male world of power-relations, and that a more inclusive human language of influence, encouragement and inspiration would be more acceptable to everyone and more likely to win the assent of minds as well as hearts.[23]

This brief sketch indicates how the authority of the Bible has been undermined. The modern emphasis on autonomy, suspicion of the past, the gulf between modern and ancient society and cultures, the uncovering of the Bible's human origins by modern biblical scholarship, the decline of denominational structures, the plurality of the biblical writings, and the questioning of the applicability of 'authority' to the Bible have led to a widespread uneasiness about the notion of biblical authority in Western society.

At first sight, the most straightforward way out of the difficulties associated with the concept of authority might seem to be to abandon the concept altogether and search for more adequate models of scripture. This is the approach adopted by James Barr, who prefers to speak in terms of the *function* rather than the authority of the Bible.[24] Similarly, Edward Farley critiques the 'house of authority' in which theology has traditionally been done and offers a 'theological criteriology outside the house of authority' which understands the Bible as a normative sedimentation of ecclesial existence.[25] As Goldingay points out, however,

> escape from the models turns out to be more difficult

[23] Clines, *What Does Eve Do to Help?*, p. 48.

[24] Barr, *Bible in the Modern World*, esp. pp. 30–4, 180–1. See also David H. Kelsey, *The Uses of Scripture in Recent Theology* (London: SCM Press, 1975), esp. pp. 182–204.

[25] Edward Farley, *Ecclesial Reflection* (Philadelphia: Fortress, 1982), see esp. pp. 272–81.

> than it looks. 'Function' is rather vague, and while Farley demolishes 'the house of authority' in the first part of his book, the second part is so concerned with 'norms' that he may seem to be rebuilding a not wholly dissimilar new dwelling.[26]

A more profitable approach is adopted by Goldingay, who suggests that the terms 'witness' and 'tradition' are better able than 'authority' to capture the nature of the Bible: 'if there is one overarching model for scripture, it is the witnessing tradition'.[27] The advantages of these terms Goldingay describes as follows:

> As witness, the narratives testify to events that have happened that constitute the good news their message brings. As tradition they pass on an account of events that have happened and that are important for people who have not personally experienced them.[28]

Consequently, 'The fundamental reason for acknowledging the authority of the scriptures as the expression of divine revelation and the inspired word of God is the witness they bear.[29]

While acknowledging the strength of Goldingay's argument and recognizing the appropriateness of conceiving of the Bible as 'witnessing tradition', it seems to me that this does not necessitate the abandonment of the concept of authority. The usefulness of the term 'authority' is that it expresses something concerning the nature of the relationship of human beings to the Bible. That is, in contrast to

[26] Goldingay, *Models for Scripture*, p. 12.
[27] Ibid., p. 17.
[28] Ibid., p. 16.
[29] Ibid., p. 28.

'witness' and 'tradition', 'authority' is a relational term and articulates the (possible) nature of the interaction between reader and sacred text. The application of the concept 'authority' to the Bible expresses the insight that the Bible makes some sort of claim upon human beings and that the correct response to these ancient writings, or rather to that which they mediate, is one of obedience.

Goldingay's other point, that 'authority' is applied in the Bible not to texts but exclusively to persons, does not necessarily count against our discussion of the Bible in terms of authority. Although the term 'authority' may not be applied overtly to scripture within the biblical writings, it seems to be strongly implied by Jesus' use of the phrase 'it is written' when citing the Old Testament (Matt 4.4, 7, 10) and by the frequent appeals of the New Testament writers to the Old Testament. Furthermore, terms drawn from outside scripture may capture something essential about the nature of scripture that is implied, if not explictly stated, in scripture. As Goldingay himself admits, 'Sometimes we need terms from outside scripture if we are to pursue the task of reflective theological analysis of scripture's actual statements.'[30] Indeed, we could argue that if we were only to employ terms specifically mentioned in scripture, we should have to dispense with such central Christian terms as 'incarnation' and 'Trinity', neither of which appear in the Bible. It thus seems legitimate and indeed appropriate to apply the term 'authority' to the Bible as a whole if it is able to capture an essential feature of the biblical writings.

Finally, the concept of authority would seem to be required by the Christian conviction that God has revealed himself in the Person of his Son Jesus Christ. As Lash points out,

[30] Ibid., p. 4.

> As christians we are surely committed to some form of the belief that a uniquely authoritative word has been definitively and irrevocably spoken, at one time and one place in the past, in the life, words, deeds and death of one man. As a result, we seem to be committed to the belief that the words which witness to that word . . . must continue to be heard by us as authoritative, in our very different time and place.[31]

In my opinion, the problem is not the alleged inapplicability of 'authority' to the Bible, but, as we shall go on to see, isolating the *type* of authority the Bible possesses. In this study I wish to show that it is still valid to speak in terms of the authority of the Bible, and to show that this authority is best defended by means of a theology of inspiration.

The meanings of authority

Before we can embark upon the task of constructing a theology of inspiration, however, we must clarify the nature of authority, for confusion as to the meaning of this term has seriously hampered debate on the nature of *biblical* authority. We should above all heed Lash's warning that, 'For too long christian debates about authority (which must, in the last resort, be debates about the authority of God) have implied, however unwittingly, a thoroughly unchristian concept of God.'[32] We must ensure that any concept of the authority of the Bible that we

[31] Lash, *Voices of Authority*, p. 62.
[32] Ibid., p. 12.

develop does justice to the nature of God.[33] To quote Lash again:

> As christians we should continually be asking ourselves the question: What concept of God, and of God's relationship to man, is implied by that notion of authority (whatever it may be) which we regard as relevant to, or appropriate for, our discussion of the christian quest for truth – for right belief and right action?[34]

We need therefore to pin down as firmly as possible which of the many meanings and applications of 'authority' is appropriate to the Bible, before we can begin to talk meaningfully of biblical authority.

This attempt to distinguish between different aspects of the concept of authority has been criticized in some quarters. Barr comments that, 'There is . . . little chance that such fine distinctions could be sustained in ordinary usage'[35] and that,

> If the term 'authority' is so defined as to make it more flexible and to increase the emphasis on free decision and acceptance, this may only create a confusion or produce something which the average person will not recognize as 'authority' at all.[36]

[33] We shall leave to one side the question of the relationship between the authority of the Bible and the authority of the Church. Interesting though this issue is, its importance and complexity would require another monograph if we were to do it justice.

[34] Lash, *Voices of Authority*, p. 10.

[35] Barr, *Bible in the Modern World*, p. 26. A similar point is made by the World Council of Churches, *Faith and Order: Louvain 1971. Study Reports and Documents* (Faith and Order Paper 59; Geneva, 1971), 14.

[36] Barr, *Bible in the Modern World*, pp. 26–7.

Barr also goes on to point out that 'the dominant strain in the authority concept is a legal one' and that this is how the term has generally been applied in the West and the way in which the average hearer interprets it. Such a hearer, Barr continues, will 'feel that he is being tricked with double talk', if the term is used in a way that does not correspond to its 'hard', legal sense.

It seems to me that we are by no means obliged to accept Barr's attempt to reduce the concept of authority to a homogeneity. There is a very simple reason for this: the concept of authority is not homogeneous but is highly complex and has a variety of different nuances. Lash points out that the degree of authority a statement possesses can be

> plotted along a line between two extreme positions. At one end of the line, a statement may be 'heard' as authoritative . . . simply because it convinces us on its own terms. It immediately and compellingly strikes us as true . . . At the other end of the line, a statement may be 'heard' as authoritative, regardless of its content, *simply* because we recognise and acknowledge the 'authority' of the one who utters it.[37]

As we shall go on to see, there are different forms of authority and a diversity of contexts within which authority can be exercised. To complain of attempts to separate out the different meanings and applications of authority is to fail to appreciate the complexity and richness of the concept. It is thus important that we attempt at the outset to establish which understanding or understandings of authority are applicable to the Bible. Only then will we be in a position to consider the grounds for and validity of this authority.

[37] Lash, *Voices of Authority*, p. 8 (original emphasis).

Authority, authoritarianism, and power

There is an unfortunate tendency to equate authority with authoritarianism or, to put it another way, to understand authority as the exercise of power. Authority, authoritarianism and power, however, are terms with distinct meanings. Jüngel points out that the term 'authoritarian' describes 'those authorities which impose their demands by force, or attempt to do so, *without* making the necessity of their claim *so evident* to those on whom they make it that those persons can *freely accept* it'. The term 'authoritative', on the other hand, denotes 'authorities which enforce their demands by making the rightfulness of those demands *so evident* to those on whom the demands are made that (while realizing the possibility of objection) those persons admit the rightfulness of the demands'.[38]

A similar distinction is made by Dulles and Lash between authority and power. Dulles points out that although authority and power 'may in fact coincide, so that power is exercised by way of authority, and authority makes itself felt as power', the two terms are not identical. 'Authority', Dulles writes, 'is always a moral relationship between free and rational subjects', whereas 'power . . . may be sheerly physical' and 'can be exerted by dead matter as well as by persons; and it can be used upon lifeless things, animals, or insane and unwilling subjects'.[39] A similar argument is advanced by Lash, who writes:

> Whereas the concept of authority always refers to a moral relationship between free and rational subjects,

[38] Eberhard Jüngel, Gerhard Krodel, René Marlé and John D. Zizioulas, 'Four preliminary considerations on the concept of authority', in *Ecumenical Review* xxi (1969), 150–66; 150; original emphasis.

[39] Avery Dulles, *The Survival of Dogma* (Garden City, NY: Doubleday, 1971), p. 80.

> the concept of power may refer to sheerly physical, material relationships. I may have the power to kick a stone, or a donkey, but it would be odd to speak of my having authority over them.[40]

Like Dulles, Lash points out that the concept of authority contains a moral dimension that is absent from the concept of power:

> To speak of authority is usually to speak of moral entitlement. From the mere fact that I have another person 'in my power', it does not necessarily follow that they are subject to my authority. Correlatively we may speak of persons acting with authority in situations where they are powerless to produce the results they intend.[41]

As Dulles puts it, 'Thus a person may have authority without power or power without authority.'[42]

Of these three terms, 'authority', 'authoritarianism' and 'power', it seems clear that 'authoritarianism' and 'power' are inadequate expressions of the nature of biblical authority. The authority of the Bible does not involve the exercise of power, but involves a moral relationship with the reader. Its divine status cannot be forced upon individuals without violating the autonomy with which

[40] Lash, *Voices of Authority*, p. 16.

[41] Ibid. Cunliffe-Jones seems to be making a similar point in his distinction between final authority, educative authority and the authority of power: 'There is the final authority in which right and power are united, there is the educative authority which has right so far as its truth has not been assimilated, but no power, and there is the authority of power, hardly to be found in complete isolation from right, but not primarily dependent upon it'. H. Cunliffe-Jones, *The Authority of the Biblical Revelation* (London: James Clarke & Co., 1945), p. 13.

[42] Dulles, *Survival of Dogma*, p. 80.

God has endowed human beings. As Cunliffe-Jones puts it,

> God does not ask for a coerced love, but for the free homage of man in trust to his Creator and Redeemer. The dragooning of men into faith is no assertion of the authority of God, but the attempt to force in the worst possible way that positive freedom which God desires for man.[43]

The Bible is not authoritarian, but it is authoritative for those who freely accept it as the Word of God.

Normative and causative authority

A *normative authority* (*auctoritas normativa*) is one which provides a standard or norm by which something can be measured and/or judged. Thus in industry, for example, norms are essential for ensuring consistency of production. Lack of norms would result in an unacceptable variation in the quality of the goods manufactured.

The Bible quite clearly possesses normative authority in this sense for both the Churches and individual Christians, for it provides the pre-eminent standard by which Christian teaching and living is judged. The Bible is both the starting-point and the governing principle of Christian theology and the source for and basis of the Christian understanding of human existence. This normative status stems from the Bible's unique witness to the preparation for and coming of Christ, and to the events which led to the foundation of the Church. As the unique witness to the foundational events of Christianity, the Bible is the criterion and norm of Christian doctrine.

Causative authority (*auctoritas causativa*) is, as Härle

[43] Cunliffe-Jones, *Authority of the Biblical Revelation*, p. 18.

puts it, 'that authority through which scripture produces and establishes the assent of the rational human being to the contents of the faith'.[44] Härle further points out that this understanding of causative authority is closely connected with another characteristic traditionally ascribed to the Bible, namely its *efficacia*, that is, its effectiveness as a source of illumination, conversion and the salvation of human beings. Causative authority is more fundamental than normative authority. It is situated in the Bible's capacity to address human beings in such a way that they come to faith. It is this capacity that enables the Bible to be the Word of God and it is the capacity of the Bible to evoke faith that constitutes the only proof that it *is* the Word of God. The fundamental question is how this causative authority is grounded. What are our reasons for considering the Bible to be a causative authority?

Executive and non-executive authority

The political scientist Richard T. De George provides a useful definition of authority in his comprehensive study, *The Nature and Limits of Authority*. He writes: 'someone or something (X) is an authority if he (she, or it) stands in relation to someone else (Y) as superior stands to inferior with respect to some realm, field, or domain (R)'.[45] There are thus two core ideas present in the concept of authority. The first is that authority involves a relationship between two parties. The second is that this is an unequal relationship in which one of the two parties is inferior or subordinate in some way to the other. This basic meaning of authority as a relationship between two unequal

[44] Wilfried Härle, *Dogmatik* (Berlin: de Gruyter, 1995), p. 115.

[45] Richard T. De George, *The Nature and Limits of Authority* (Lawrence, KS: Kansas University Press, 1985), p. 14.

partners can be broken down into two major subdivisions. De George distinguishes between what he terms 'executive' and 'nonexecutive' authority, which he defines as follows: 'In general, an executive authority has the right or power to act for or on someone else. A nonexecutive authority does not.'[46] An example of executive authority is the authority held by a military commander over the soldiers under his or her command. The commander has the authority to dictate the soldiers' actions and to compel them to carry out his or her orders. Similarly, the President or Prime Minister has executive authority in that he or she has the power to determine government policy and guide the life of the nation. Now the sources of the authority of the military commander and the President may differ and the limitations placed upon their authority may vary, but the common feature of the authority of both individuals is that they possess the capacity to impose their wills upon other human beings. Somebody who has non-executive authority, on the other hand, has no power to impose his or her will upon others. Examples of non-executive authority are what De George terms 'epistemic' and 'exemplary' authority. 'An epistemic authority', he writes, 'is an authority in a field of knowledge.'[47] To put it in its most simple and straightforward form, someone has or is an epistemic authority because he or she knows more about a particular subject than his or her fellow human beings. Professors of chemistry, for example, are epistemic authorities to their students by virtue of their superior knowledge of chemistry. An exemplary authority, on the other hand, is someone who is imitated by others. If other human beings

[46] Ibid., p. 22. De George also provides a more formal definition of executive authority: 'Executive authority is the right or power of someone (X) to do something (S) in some realm, field, or domain (R), in a context (C)' (p. 17).

[47] Ibid., p. 22.

believe that a particular individual is worthy of emulation, then they are implicitly acknowledging that individual's authority. In neither epistemic nor exemplary authority, however, does the 'authoritative' individual possess *executive* power. The epistemic authority of, say, professors of chemistry does not give them the power to command their students. The professor's knowledge of chemistry does not entail, De George writes, 'the right or power to act for or on someone else'. The authority of the professor is thus non-executive.

Is the Bible's authority executive or non-executive? It seems clear that the Bible is a non-executive authority. It is non-executive because although it may record divine commands, it does not itself command. The Bible is rather an epistemic authority, for it provides us with knowledge about religious matters. As Krodel points out, 'The authority of the Bible can also be understood in terms of *expertise* in religious matters. An expert in a particular field *is* an authority on a given subject, though he may not *have* authority over institutions or people.'[48] The Bible has epistemic authority because it provides us with knowledge which we cannot obtain from any other source. The Bible, however, is an epistemic authority of a very special and unusual kind. According to De George, 'Someone is an epistemic authority by virtue of knowledge and trustworthiness, which can, in principle, be checked independently.'[49] This presents us with a problem in the case of the Bible, for its claims cannot be checked independently. Although the various biblical writings can be subject to historical-critical analysis, the doctrinal claims the Bible makes cannot be tested by any external authority, for if

[48] Jüngel, Krodel, Marlé and Zizioulas, 'Four preliminary considerations', 154 (original emphasis).
[49] De George, *Nature and Limits*, p. 235.

these doctrines are indeed from God, then there is no higher authority by which they can be judged. An important question is thus how we can ground the epistemic authority of the Bible.

De facto, legitimate and de jure authority

A further important aspect of the concept of authority is the question of the justification of authority. This, too, is a complex question, for an individual's authority can have a variety of different levels of justification, depending on the nature of those over whom he or she has authority and the nature of the realm or context in which authority is exercised.

A 'de facto authority' is an authority acknowledged as an authority by others. As De George puts it, 'Let us call X a de facto authority if he is recognized as such by some Y who acts appropriately in response to X.' De facto authority, De George writes, is the weakest sense in which the term authority can be used. It merely acknowledges that one person may accept another as an authority and 'leave[s] open the question of whether it is ever right or justifiable . . . for one person to be an authority for another'.[50] According to De George, de facto authority can vary both in extent and intensity. He writes: 'The extent of [X's] authority is a function of the number of persons for whom he is an authority . . . Intensity refers to the degree of acceptance of the authority by those subject to authority.' Thus, to take De George's own example, 'The extent of the authority of the professor is greater than that of most parents and less than that of the president.'[51] On the other hand, 'a parent's authority over his young children would be more intense

[50] Ibid., p. 18.
[51] Ibid., p. 20.

than a professor's over his students if the children believed firmly what was said to them by their parents just because they said it, while the professor's students were inclined to believe what he said, but not very firmly'.[52]

The problem with de facto authority is its high degree of subjectivity, for it is dependent upon an individual's choice to accept another human being as an authority. For an authority to be more than merely a de facto authority, it is necessary that the subjective decision of the individual to accept X as an authority has some sort of objective justification. De George speaks of this in terms of the *validity* of authority. He writes: 'I shall refer to someone as a "valid authority" if he fulfills some additional criterion (CR) that is specified as necessary and sufficient in order for someone to be an authority in a strong or prescriptive sense.'[53] The central question is: What is this criterion? On what grounds can an individual's authority be based?

In his attempt to answer these questions De George introduces the concepts of 'legitimate' and 'de jure' authority. 'An authority [is] a legitimate authority', he writes, 'if he is a grounded authority . . . If X's authority is not grounded, he is an illegitimate authority.'[54] There can be many different ways in which an authority can be grounded and acquire legitimacy. It may be grounded in alleged divine fiat, as has often been the case with monarchies, or it may be grounded in the alleged will of the people, as is the case with democracies. Others may claim 'nature' or 'reason' as the justification for their authority, claiming that they are acting in accordance or in harmony with 'natural law' or with the laws of reason. The important point to note is that authority must be grounded

[52] Ibid.
[53] Ibid., p. 18.
[54] Ibid., p. 19.

in some reality external to the individual who claims authority and the sphere in which this authority is exercised if it is to count as legitimate.

De jure authority is the form of authority which an individual has, according to De George, 'if he holds his position of authority and exercises his authority in accordance with a certain set of rules or specified procedures, which are frequently legal'. A de jure authority is not necessarily identical with a legitimate authority, however. De George writes: 'Authority may be de jure but not grounded (and hence not legitimate) if the legal framework or other set of rules is not grounded or justified; and it may be grounded but not de jure if its exercise is justified though contrary to the rules or laws.'[55]

Which, if any, of these various conceptions of authority is appropriate to the Bible? The first question we should ask is whether the Bible is an authority at all. The answer to this question must surely be 'yes', for it is uncontroversial that there are many people who accept that the Bible has authority over their lives. The Bible, then, clearly has de facto authority, since it is an authority for all those – churches and individual believers – who accept it as authoritative. This maps on to the theological conception of the Bible as *auctoritas normativa*. Many modern scholars have been happy to settle for this understanding of the Bible's authority.[56]

The problem facing the Christian theologian, however, and the problem I wish to address in this study, is that of

[55] Ibid., p. 19.

[56] See, for example, Charles Wood, *The Formation of Christian Understanding: An Essay in Theological Hermeneutics* (Philadelphia: Westminster, 1981); Kelsey, *Uses of Scripture in Recent Theology*, pp. 97–8; Robert Gnuse, *The Authority of the Bible: Theories of Inspiration, Revelation, and the Canon of Scripture* (New York/Mahwah: Paulist Press, 1985), p. 123.

showing that the Bible is more than just a de facto authority. One of the claims traditionally made for the Bible is that it speaks to *all* human beings and not just to those who consider themselves Christians. That is, it is claimed that the Bible is a *universal* authority. Indeed, if the Bible is not to be reduced to being merely a rule book or manifesto of the 'Christian club', then such a claim is absolutely necessary. We need to show why and how the Bible has the potential to address all human beings. In addition to this, one of the reasons for the de facto acceptance of the Bible is the belief on the part of those who accept its authority that its significance extends far beyond the boundaries of the Church. To put it another way, the acceptance of the authority of the Bible is possible only because believers believe it to be grounded, that is, to have its source, in God. If they are right, the Bible has more than merely de facto authority; it has universal authority. As Pannenberg points out, 'The term God is used meaningfully only if one means by it the power that determines everything that exists.'[57] The universality of the Bible stems from this. The Bible speaks of God and, if there is a God, then as the power that determines all that exists, God's claim upon human beings will not be limited only to those within the Christian circle, but will be applicable to all human beings. Texts which speak of God and communicate his will for humankind will thus – at least theoretically – be addressed to all human beings and not just to those within the circle of faith. Furthermore, as Pannenberg points out, 'Scripture speaks of the creation of the world, of man, and of God's history with the human race from the beginning of the world to its coming end. Such statements claim universality.'[58] Whether all human

[57] Pannenberg, 'Crisis of the scripture principle', p. 1.
[58] Ibid., p. 3.

beings respond to the divine address which believers are convinced resides in the Bible is another matter, but Christianity is arguably committed to the claim that the Bible has universal application and that its significance is not restricted exclusively to Christians. The problem facing those who subscribe to this view is that of showing this to those outside the Christian circle. The problem, to employ De George's terminology, is that of showing that the Bible is a valid authority.

Now the concepts that De George employs with regard to the validity of authority are 'de jure' and 'legitimacy'. Are these of any assistance in our discussion of biblical authority? Our answer to this question will depend upon whether we regard the Bible as a purely human book or as originating in some way with God. As De George points out, 'Human authority can be objectified and embodied in human products – books or laws, traditions or institutions.'[59] The Bible can thus be said to have de jure authority in so far as it is vested with legal power by human beings. There have been periods in human history where this was the case and vestiges of it can still be seen in the custom of swearing an oath on the Bible before taking the stand at a trial. But even in these cases the authority vested in the Bible is not purely human, at least not from the perspective of those who vest it with authority, for the reason that they vest it with de jure authority is that they believe it to be God's Word. Thus if we take the divine origins of the Bible seriously, then it cannot really of itself be said to possess de jure authority. It possesses de jure authority only in so far as it is vested with such authority by human beings. In addition to this, there are features of the Bible that preclude its authority from being described as de jure. Firstly, if the Bible is indeed God's Word, then it

[59] De George, *Nature and Limits*, p. 16.

cannot be described in terms of de jure authority because there is no set of rules to which the Bible can be legitimately subjected and according to which its authority can be measured, for there is no authority higher than God. Secondly, the Bible cannot have de jure authority because it stands over and against society in judgement on it. This does not mean that there is no overlap or compatibility between the Bible and society's norms and laws. There clearly is an overlap, which is hardly surprising in view of the fact that Western society has been heavily influenced by the Bible. But the crucial fact to note is that the Bible is not reducible to society's norms.

External and internal authority

A further important distinction is between what we might term 'external' and 'internal' authority. External authority is based on an appeal to external factors for its justification. Zizioulas points out that,

> All classical definitions of authority are based on the latin idea of *auctoritas* and share a common characteristic: they presuppose authority as an *external claim to submission*. This claim is 'external' in the sense that it is an objective reality imposing itself upon the subject, i.e. a claim coming from an objectified being or from a *principle* or *value* which may not be identical with a personal being but which represents, nevertheless, an objectified reality itself . . . Its expression usually takes a *juridical form* consisting of a demand for *obedience* to certain orders which must be fulfilled, or of a demand for an attitude of total submission.[60]

[60] Jüngel, Krodel, Marlé and Zizioulas, 'Four preliminary considerations', 160–1; original emphasis.

This type of authority seems to correspond to what De George calls 'conventional authority', which is authority that 'derives from a particular position: the office of president, of a judge, or of a legislator'.[61] Internal authority, on the other hand, is not dependent on the appeal to external powers but resides within the object or person of authority. This type of authority is described by De George as 'natural authority', which is 'that authority which accrues to a person because of natural qualities, such as leadership, strength, or personal magnetism'.[62]

Sabatier understands this distinction between what we have termed external and internal authority to apply to the relationship between theology and the other academic disciplines. In theology, he writes, it is the 'method of authority' which reigns, the chief characteristic of which is

> to base all judgment of doctrine upon the exterior marks of its origin and the trustworthiness of those who promulgated it. In religion this method appeals to miracles, which accredit God's messengers to men, and stamp their words or writings with the divine imprint.[63]

Sabatier goes on to point out that this understanding of authority is based on

> the axiom that it is reasonable and just that human reason should subordinate itself to the divine reason, should indeed be silent and humble before it. All reasoning of this kind avowedly or tacitly implies on

[61] De George, *Nature and Limits*, p. 23.
[62] Ibid.
[63] Auguste Sabatier, *The Religions of Authority and the Religions of the Spirit* (London: Williams & Norgate, 1904), p. xxi.

> the part of the thinking subject a declaration of incompetence, and as a consequence a conscious or unconscious act of abdication.[64]

Sabatier contrasts this theological method with 'the modern experimental method', which 'puts us in immediate contact with reality, and teaches us to judge of a doctrine only according to its intrinsic value, directly manifested to the mind in the degree of its evidence'.[65] The method of authority, as Sabatier sees it, is thus an abdication of autonomy, whereas the methods employed by the other academic disciplines respect human autonomy. Sabatier sees it as vital for the survival of theology that it should abandon the 'method of authority' and adopt the experimental, perhaps we should rather say 'experiential', method of the sciences. He warns:

> If theology persists in subjecting itself to an ancient method from which all other disciplines have freed themselves, it will not only find itself in sterile isolation, but it will expose itself to the irrefutable denials and unchallengeable judgments of a reason always more and more independent and certain of itself.[66]

Although we should undoubtedly heed Sabatier's warning that theology must cease to appeal to exterior authority and make greater use of the experimental method, we must also take seriously the weaknesses of his exposition. Sabatier's identification of theology with external authority and the sciences with internal authority is too simplistic. In

64 Ibid., p. xxii.
65 Ibid., p. xxi.
66 Ibid., p. xxiii.

reality both types of authority are applicable to theology and, as Lash points out, it is important that we should strike a balance between them.

> If we appeal too exclusively to internal, material criteria of authority, then we shall be in danger of substituting our standards and our experience for the authority of God; and thus in danger of reducing christianity to no more than another variant of liberal humanism. Nevertheless, it is also true that, if we appeal too exclusively to external, formal criteria of authority, then we shall be implicitly appealing to the authority of a God who is simply alien to human experience, who simply contradicts it and stands over against it.[67]

The limitations of authority

Finally, we should say something about the limitations of authority. The concern among writers on the authority of the Bible has usually been to establish as conclusively as possible the uniquely high status of the Bible; but part of the task, if we are to do justice to the nature of the Bible, must also be to establish as clearly as possible the *limits* of biblical authority. In non-theological contexts authority is usually restricted to a specific realm or sphere. A professor of chemistry may be an authority in her subject but she has no authority when she moves outside this sphere. Her status as a figure of authority in the world of chemistry gives her no right or power, for example, to carry out medical operations or teach a foreign language. Similarly, the authority a military commander has over his soldiers gives him no right of command over civilians, at least not

[67] Lash, *Voices of Authority*, p. 12.

until they lose their civilian status by being drafted into the army. Authority, then, is usually limited in scope. It is restricted to a specific realm or context and it is only in very exceptional circumstances, such as an absolute monarchy or a totalitarian state, that a single individual may claim and seek to exercise absolute authority, i.e., authority with regard to everything. Is such absolute authority applicable to the Bible? The answer to this question must surely be 'no'. The Bible cannot be regarded as an absolute authority because it is not an authority in respect of everything. There are clearly areas of experience and knowledge that the Bible simply does not address. The Bible is, for example, clearly not an authority on chemistry, methods of industrial production, artistic techniques and so on. It is possible, however, to speak of the Bible's *universal* authority, and perhaps it is this that people really mean when they speak of the absolute authority of the Bible. To speak of the Bible's universal authority does not mean that the Bible has authority in every realm, but that, as we saw earlier, the Bible addresses every human being.

If it is to be true both to the nature of God and to human autonomy, such authority as the Bible possesses cannot be authoritarian or executive. The authority of the Bible cannot be forced upon human beings without injuring human autonomy and making impossible the free acceptance of the divine gift offered in the Bible. If the Bible is to be a liberating gift rather than an oppressive violator of human freedom, its authority cannot be understood in authoritarian terms.

The Bible clearly has normative and de facto authority, for it is accepted as authoritative within the Christian community and regarded as normative for Christian existence. Those who accept the authority of the Bible do so because it possesses epistemic and exemplary authority.

The Bible possesses epistemic authority by virtue of its provision of knowledge of the foundational events of the Christian faith, an insight into the nature of God and a portrayal of the nature of human existence before God. If we wish to know about the person of Jesus and the events that led to the founding of the Church, the Bible is the primary source. It also possesses exemplary authority by virtue of the fact that it provides examples of human behaviour and models of human existence in the presence of God. But the function of the Bible is more than merely that of providing information about events in the distant past. The biblical writings have been preserved because their compilers and those who have handed them down to subsequent generations have desired to 'keep and make the revelation alive' for future generations. The biblical writers aim at inculcating and sustaining faith. Consequently, the Bible is felt by Christians to possess causative authority, for it is believed to possess – through the agency of the Holy Spirit – the power to bring to faith those who hear and read it.

The problem is that of justifying these claims. To employ De George's terminology, the challenge is to show that the Bible is a legitimate and valid authority; i.e., that the authority of the Bible is not merely de facto but is grounded in some way. Traditionally, the authoritative status of the Bible has been grounded by appealing to the concepts of revelation, the Word of God and inspiration.[68] Of these

[68] Authority is the primary concept, whereas such concepts as revelation, Word of God and inspiration are secondary concepts. The latter constitute attempts to provide justification for the former. When the question is raised as to why the Bible is authoritative, an answer is provided by pointing to the fact that it is God's revelation or that it is the Word of God or that it is inspired. The question of the Bible's authority, then, can be answered only by turning to a second set of concepts. The reverse, however, does not apply. If we wish to justify the claim that the

three terms we choose to centre our discussion on the concept of inspiration. The concepts of revelation and Word of God are ill-suited to capture the nature of the reader's relationship to the Bible and his or her grounds for accepting it as the authoritative revelation of God's will. They may well be useful concepts once the individual has accepted the authority of the Bible, but they both say little about the processes by which the believer arrives at acceptance of biblical authority. What we need is some understanding of the mechanism that enables the human being to see in this diverse collection of texts the expression of the divine will. For that we require a conception that is able to do justice not only to the contents of the Bible, but also to the reader's interaction with the biblical texts. It seems to me that the most useful tool for achieving this is the concept of inspiration.

In considering the question of the inspiration of scripture, however, we must not be too ambitious. The relation between God and the biblical texts is, and most probably will always remain, a mystery. As Farrer comments with regard to Paul and John, 'the moving of these men's minds, or of any men's minds, by divine direction is in any case a profound and invisible mystery, as is the whole relation of the creature to the creator'.[69] The task is not so much to 'explain' inspiration but to bring out the existential significance of the Bible. As we shall go on to see, it is in

Bible is inspired or is the Word of God, we cannot say that it is these things because it has authority (cf. Gnuse, *Authority of the Bible*, pp. 64–5). It is possible, of course, to proceed from the formulation of, say, a doctrine of inspiration to the consideration that the Bible has authority, but this is a tacit admission of the primacy of the concept of authority, for it implies that the concept of authority is the goal towards which the theory of inspiration is directed and in which it culminates.

[69] Austin Farrer, *The Glass of Vision* (Westminster: Dacre Press, 1948), p. 113.

the life-transforming power of the biblical texts that their inspiration lies.

The meanings of inspiration

To justify our employment of the concept of inspiration as the basis of our discussion of biblical authority, it is necessary to identify the central features of inspiration. This is not an easy task, however, for, as Timothy Clark comments in his discussion of literary theories of inspiration, inspiration comprises 'a tight knot of different, even contradictory, claims about subjectivity, value and productivity'.[70] The following is an attempt to untie this knot and isolate the characteristics of biblical inspiration.

Inspiration has what we might loosely term an 'objective' and a 'subjective' dimension. By the objective dimension of inspiration I mean that to speak of the Bible as inspired includes the claim that 'inspiration' is not merely a value judgement on the part of the reader of the Bible but is a feature of the biblical texts. This 'objective' inspiration of the Bible is the consequence of the alleged divine input into the biblical writings. God, it is claimed, is involved in some way in the composition of the biblical texts and, as a consequence of this divine involvement, these are held to be objectively inspired. By subjective inspiration I mean that 'inspiration' says something about the way human beings are, or can be, involved with texts. That is, there are resources in 'inspired' texts that can – if allowed – have a qualitative impact on human existence. The term 'inspiration' in its subjective sense, then, expresses the impact of

[70] Timothy Clark, *The Theory of Inspiration: Composition as a crisis of subjectivity in Romantic and post-Romantic writing* (Manchester: Manchester University Press, 1997), p. 3.

the biblical texts on the reader. The reader, it is claimed, is inspired when reading these texts or, alternatively, the reader must be inspired if he or she is to accept these texts as inspired. This type of inspiration is important for making clear that inspiration cannot be reduced *exclusively* to a feature of the text. The acceptance of a text as inspired involves a subjective response on the part of the reader. Without such a response the hearer or reader of the Bible is unable to perceive the objective inspiration of the biblical texts. Subjective inspiration is thus essential if we are to account for the phenomenon that one individual is able to regard the Bible as inspired, while another treats the Bible merely as a collection of ancient texts, perhaps worthy of study as interesting historical and literary documents, but otherwise of no greater significance or relevance than any other set of ancient writings.

Objective and subjective inspiration are linked through the role played in both forms of inspiration by the Holy Spirit. On the one hand, the Holy Spirit is understood to prompt and guide the authors of the Old and New Testaments in the composition of the biblical writings. On the other hand, the Holy Spirit is held to be responsible for enabling the reader to encounter the Bible as God's Word. Calvin describes this latter form of inspiration as the 'internal testimony of the Holy Spirit' ('testimonium internum Spiritus Sancti').[71] He writes:

> For as God alone can properly bear witness to his own words, so these words will not obtain full credit in the hearts of men, until they are sealed by the inward testimony of the Spirit. The same Spirit, therefore, who spoke by the mouth of the prophets, must

[71] Calvin, *Institutes of the Christian Religion*, trans. Henry Beveridge, (London: James Clarke, 1949), I. vii. 4; cf. III. ii. 33–4.

> penetrate our hearts, in order to convince us that they faithfully delivered the message with which they were divinely intrusted.[72]

Without this inner testimony of the Spirit the Bible, regardless of the processes of inspiration that have brought it into existence, cannot speak religiously and spiritually to the reader. Inspiration, then, is not limited merely to the processes by which the biblical texts came into existence, but must also be present in the reader's relation to the text if these texts are truly to be inspired for that reader.

We can qualify the concept of inspiration still further by distinguishing between 'active' and 'passive', 'causative' and 'resultative' inspiration. In so far as someone or something inspires an other, inspiration constitutes an action in which an inspiring agent acts upon the object or recipient of this inspiring activity. Inspiration in this sense is also a cause. The inspiring agent *causes* an other to enter or acquire a state of inspiration. We can describe this type of inspiration as active and/or causative inspiration.

As well as being an activity, however, inspiration is paradoxically also a state, namely the state or condition of having been (and possibly still being) inspired. As a result of the impact upon the object or recipient of the inspiring agent's active inspiration, the object or recipient of inspiration enters the state or condition of being inspired. Inspiration in this sense is also an effect or result of the action of an inspiring agent. We can thus describe this type of inspiration as passive or resultative inspiration.

Active and passive, causative and resultative inspiration exist in a complex dialectic. Without being in an inspired state (passive inspiration), the inspiring agent cannot inspire others. That is, without being oneself inspired it is

[72] Calvin, *Institutes* I. vii. 4.

impossible to inspire others. Active inspiration would thus seem to be dependent upon passive inspiration. Yet at the same time the inspired state (passive inspiration) is the result or effect of having being inspired by an inspiring agent. Passive inspiration is thus dependent upon active inspiration, on having been inspired by another.

It is this complex dialectic of objective and subjective, active and passive, causative and resultative inspiration that accounts for the ambivalence of authorship that is a feature of 'inspired' writings. On the one hand, the author feels him or herself to be the passive recipient of inspiration bestowed upon the author from an external source. On the other hand, that very same writer has an active role in inspiring others through the writings he or she has produced as a result of having been inspired.

It is precisely its composition as a complex interrelationship of objectivity and subjectivity, activity and passivity, cause and effect, that makes the concept of inspiration both an elusive term and simultaneously a useful tool for considering the nature of biblical authority. The Bible is authoritative because those involved in its production have been 'inspired'. Simultaneously, the reader or hearer of the Bible must also be inspired in order to be able to receive and accept the Bible as authoritative. The concept of inspiration may thus provide a useful bridge between the author and the reader of the Bible which allows us to speak of both as inspired and of the axis of this inspiration as being the Bible. It is this ability to encompass the objective and subjective dimensions of the Bible that makes the concept of inspiration the most useful vehicle for consideration of the nature of the authority of the Bible. Before we unpack these ideas, however, we must examine the resources at our disposal and consider the various theories of inspiration that have been developed in answer to the question: Why and how is the Bible authoritative?

2

Word-centred theories of inspiration

It is a remarkable fact that the Church has never felt it necessary to fix as orthodox a particular understanding of the Bible. The Church Fathers did not have a fixed, authoritative doctrine of inspiration, nor was a particular understanding of inspiration elevated to credal status. There are several reasons for this. First, the authority of scripture was subsumed under the authority of the Church. That is, the authority of scripture was only one aspect of the authority of the Church, which could also appeal to the rule of faith and the tradition it believed to have been handed down by Christ to the apostles and through them to the Church. Secondly, the Fathers simply took the significance and centrality of the Bible for granted. Consequently there was only limited discussion in the early Church concerning the grounds for the Bible's significance and centrality.

It is, however, no longer the case that the authoritative and inspired status of the Bible can be taken for granted, for the reasons outlined in the previous chapter. It is above all since the Enlightenment that the inspiration of the Bible has become a theological problem. In the modern era theories concerning the inspiration of scripture have traditionally been divided into two groups, namely what are loosely termed 'conservative' and 'liberal' approaches. These divisions are the consequence of the rise of the natural sciences and biblical criticism. The rise of the scientific world-view has undermined the traditional view that God intervenes in the natural order and has replaced many supernatural explanations for dramatic occurrences in nature with explanations that do not require divine agency. God is no longer believed to be present in the thunderstorm or the earthquake. This makes it difficult to take many of the biblical accounts literally, especially those which, for example, view natural disasters as God's punishment for sin. Similarly, the development of biblical criticism has revealed that the Bible contains what appear to be inconsistencies or errors and has also drawn attention to the close relationship between the Bible and other ancient Near Eastern literature. Furthermore, it is possible to provide purely cultural, historical, and sociological explanations for the contents of the biblical writings which explain those contents without needing reference to any divine initiative. Indeed, some scholars would argue that such a view of the origins of the Bible is better able to deal with the realities of the biblical text than theories based on divine intervention.

There are three ways of meeting this challenge to the concept of inspiration. One way is to abandon the concept altogether. We shall consider this approach in the final section of the next chapter. The other two approaches attempt to find some way of retaining the concept. The most vigorous of these two approaches – the so-called 'conservative' approach – remains in many respects in a pre-Enlightenment position. In its most extreme, fundamentalist forms it denies the validity and veracity of many modern scientific insights and rejects the results of modern biblical scholarship. Even in its more moderate forms, where the results of modern science and biblical scholarship are taken more seriously, the conservative approach clings to the belief that God intervenes directly in the world and attempts to reconcile the results of modern science with this basic belief.

The second approach, which is usually known as the 'liberal' approach, accepts wholeheartedly the scientific world-view and the results of biblical criticism, and attempts to adjust the concept of inspiration in their light. Very often, however, these liberal approaches resemble rearguard actions aimed at salvaging something from what appears to many critical observers to be an untenable concept.

The description of theories of inspiration in terms of whether they are 'conservative' or 'liberal' is unfortunate, however. Such terms are coloured by their political usage and, furthermore, are dependent for their use on the self-conception of those who employ them. What may seem 'conservative' to some 'liberals' may seem 'liberal' to some 'conservatives', and vice versa. Furthermore, theologians who may be 'liberal' in their treatment of the Bible may be 'conservative' in other areas of their theology. For example, with regard to the inspiration of the Bible, Charles Gore seems to belong to the 'liberal' camp, since he does not insist on the literal verbal inspiration of scripture but, as we shall see later, advances a non-verbal conception of inspiration which situates inspiration not in the words of the text but in their spiritual contents. In other respects, however, such as his Christology, Gore would seem to be more 'conservative' in outlook.

In view of the problems of the conservative–liberal distinction, William Abraham has proposed a different way of organizing theories of inspiration, namely according to whether they are 'deductive' or 'inductive'. Deductive theories of inspiration are a priori in nature. As Abraham puts it, 'A deductive type of theory begins with a basic theological claim about the meaning of inspiration and attempts to deduce from this what Scripture must be or contain.'[1] Deductive theories make certain assumptions about God and the Bible such as, for example, that God cannot lie and that the Bible is the Word of God. On the basis of such propositions it is argued that the Bible must be without error. An inductive theory, on the other hand, is a posteriori in nature. It begins with what are termed the 'phenomena' of the Bible; that is, it begins with the biblical material as we have it before us and considers whether and how this material can be said to be inspired. Proponents of this approach hold that this is the only way that we can do justice to the biblical texts, for it treats the Bible on its own terms and avoids imposing upon the Bible any preconceived view of inspiration.

Although this distinction between deductive and inductive theories of inspiration is able to capture some features of the differences between 'conservative' and 'liberal' theories of inspiration, there still remain a number of problems with it, and it is questionable whether theories of inspiration can be satisfactorily distinguished according to a deductive–inductive dichotomy. Proponents of the deductive approach do not see themselves as imposing an a priori concept of inspiration of the Bible, but as affirming an understanding which they believe to be derived from the Bible itself. As we shall see, 'deductionists' believe that the Bible itself claims that it is inspired. They would thus not conceive of themselves as imposing an a priori notion of inspiration upon the Bible but, on the contrary, as doing full justice to the phenomena of the Bible. They point to Jesus' attitude to the Old Testament and to passages in which the biblical writers affirm the authoritative status of their writings. This means that the deductive approach is not *purely* deductive, for it derives its understanding of inspiration from its reading of certain passages of scripture.

[1] Abraham, *Divine Inspiration of Holy Scripture*, p. 11.

It is true, of course, that this reading of scripture may be regarded, at least by its critics, as motivated by certain assumptions concerning the Bible that are then read into the texts that seem to support these assumptions. Either way, however, it is wrong to regard conservative theories as purely deductive. Proponents of such theories clearly believe that they are doing justice to scripture as it is, by expressing what it claims about itself.

Furthermore, even liberal 'inductionists' come to the Bible with a priori presuppositions and expectations concerning its meaning and significance. Inductionists do not come 'cold' to the Bible and then, by means of a neutral, 'inductive' assessment of the phenomena of Bible, arrive at the conclusion that texts of this nature cannot originate from human hand but only from God. Their 'inductive' treatment of the texts will be heavily influenced by, for example, whether they are Christian or non-Christian, theist or atheist. These a priori conceptions which they bring to the text will colour their understanding and interpretation of the authority and inspired status of the Bible.

To avoid these problems I propose to organize theories of inspiration according to a distinction between *word-centred* and *non-verbal* conceptions of inspiration. Word-centred theories situate the inspiration of the Bible in the words of the biblical text. Such theories are characterized by a greater emphasis on the word as the medium of divine communication. It is above all the words of the Bible which are understood as inspired. This does not mean that the message the words impart is unimportant, but that the biblical message is understood to be mediated by the words in such a way that it cannot be divorced from its verbal expression. Approaches to the Bible which attempt to translate its contents into a form more congenial to the modern mind are thus viewed with suspicion. Word-centred theories map roughly on to conservative–deductive theories of inspiration.

Non-verbal theories of inspiration situate inspiration not in the words but in some other aspect of the Bible, such as the biblical message or the processes that led to the Bible's composition. The inspiration of the biblical text is understood to be dependent on this allegedly more fundamental, non-verbal or pre-verbal inspiration. Non-verbal theories of inspiration frequently situate inspiration in the religious and moral contents of the Bible. The biblical text is then understood as merely a vehicle for the communication of these truths. These truths are not, however, tied to or dependent upon the precise wording of the biblical texts. Non-verbal theories map roughly on to liberal–inductive theories of inspiration.

There is, of course, no rigid boundary between word-centred and non-verbal theories of inspiration. Rather, they form the two poles of a sliding scale on which different theories can be placed according to the degree to which they emphasize verbal or non-verbal conceptions of inspiration. In this chapter we shall be concerned to examine the various word-centred theories of inspiration, i.e., those that are frequently designated 'conservative' and 'deductive'. These word-centred theories, it should be noted, are not mutually exclusive. Many of them overlap with each other in various ways, and what we consider here as distinct theories may in fact form components or aspects of other theories of inspiration. For the sake of clarity, however, we shall separate the various arguments that make up word-centred theories of inspiration and treat them independently of each other.

Word-centred theories of inspiration

The Bible itself says little about inspiration. That the biblical writings come from God in some way is simply taken for granted, and it is precisely for this reason that we find in the Bible no systematic presentation of inspiration and little explanation of the mechanisms by which inspiration takes place. Very occasionally certain passages of the Bible speak as if parts of the biblical writings were written directly by God. The clearest example of this is to be found in Exod 24.12: 'The Lord said to Moses, "Come up to me on the mountain, and wait there; and I will give you the tables of stone, with the law and the commandment, *which I have written for their instruction*"' (cf. Deut 5.22; emphasis added). Such claims are unusual in the Bible, however. More common is the assertion that God has made use of specially chosen human beings to carry out particular tasks. Thus God fills craftsmen and artists with his Spirit in order to enable them to make artefacts for divine worship (Exod 31.1–11). The Spirit of the Lord comes upon Gideon and Jephthah as they lead the Israelites into battle against their foes (Judg 6.34; 11.29), and we are told that God blessed Samson and 'the Spirit of the Lord began to stir in him' (Judg 13.24–25). The anointing of Saul and David as king is accompanied by the coming of the Spirit of the Lord upon the two men and, in Saul's case, the gift of prophecy (1 Sam 10.6; 16.13). Divine commissioning is frequently described in the Bible in terms of the descent of the Spirit upon the selected individual, whereupon the latter receives the ability to communicate the divine will (Num 24.2). It is above all the classical prophets of the Old Testament who are said to have or be filled and moved by the Spirit of God (Hos 9.7; Mic 3.8; Ezek 2.2; 11.5; Isa 42.1; 61.1). Isaiah looks forward to 'a shoot from the stump of Jesse', upon whom the Spirit of the Lord shall rest (Isa

11.2). It is significant that the imparting of the Divine Spirit is understood in such passages as a feature of the divine–human relationship. God inspires human beings. There is no mention here of texts being inspired. The human being is inspired to speak, rather than to write.

There is, however, another factor in the Old Testament that would later provide an important component in the development of the doctrine of scriptural inspiration. This is the custom of prefacing the proclamation of the divine message with the phrase 'Thus says the Lord', or a similar expression. David, for example, claims that 'The Spirit of the Lord speaks by me, his word is upon my tongue' (2 Sam 23.2). Ezekiel relates, 'And the Spirit of the Lord fell upon me, and he said to me, "Say, Thus says the Lord . . ."' (Ezek 11.5).[2] In view of the connection – implicit or explicit – which the Old Testament makes between reception of the Spirit and the prophet's proclamation of God's Word, it is a simple matter to extend the inspiration of the prophet first to his spoken words and subsequently to the writings in which these 'inspired words' were ultimately recorded.

The connection between inspiration and text becomes more explicit in the New Testament period. In Mark 12.36 we read that Jesus describes Ps 110.1 as having been declared by David while 'in the Spirit'. This connection between inspiration and text is at its clearest in Acts 1.16, which states that 'the *scripture* had to be fulfilled, which *the Holy Spirit* spoke beforehand by the mouth of David, concerning Judas who was guide to those who arrested Jesus' (emphasis added). Similarly, the author of the Epistle to the Hebrews prefaces his quotation of Ps 95.7–11 with the words 'as the Holy Spirit says' (Heb 3.7). In the New Testament, then, we can observe the process whereby

[2] Similar passages can be found in Isa 48.16; 61.1; Mic 3.8; and Mt 22.43; cf. 2 Pet 1.21.

inspiration becomes transferred from the speech of an inspired individual to the text in which that speech has been fixed.

The key text for theologies of inspiration, however, is 2 Tim 3.16: πᾶσα γραφὴ θεόπνευστος, literally, 'all scripture is God-breathed'. This passage has given rise to the term 'theopneustie', but it is the Latin translation of the term as 'inspiration' that has become the standard designation in Western theology for the nature of the biblical texts. The term 'inspiration' means literally 'in-breathing'. It is derived from the Latin *inspiratio*, cognates of which the Vulgate employs in the two central biblical texts for theologies of inspiration, namely 2 Tim 3.16 ('scriptura divinitus inspirata') and 2 Pet 1.21 ('Spiritu sancto inspirati, locuti sunt sancti Dei homines'). The basic meaning of inspiration is the breathing in of the divine Spirit into a human being who, under the influence of the Spirit, then communicates God's Word to his fellow human beings. These divinely inspired utterances were eventually consigned to written form either by the inspired individual himself, his followers or the community of which the inspired individual was a member. Individuals and texts can be said to be inspired if they have received God's Spirit.

The evidence of the Bible, then, indicates that (some of) those involved in the production of the biblical writings held that (some of) the texts which comprise the Bible had come about as the result of divine inspiration. The Bible is less clear, however, on the mechanism of inspiration. That is, it says little about the means by which a human being or text is made the vehicle of the Divine Spirit. This is an omission that Christian theologians have struggled to make good. The following is a brief study of word-centred theories of biblical inspiration.

Instrumental theories of inspiration

In the ancient world literary composition was commonly attributed to the agency of a deity or muse, who was held to be ultimately responsible for the creativity of the poet or seer.[3] The inspired individual was understood to be little more than a passive tool or instrument in the hands of the god or muse. Such inspiration was often accompanied and recognized by a dramatic physical transformation. The god or muse was held to induce in the inspired individual an ecstatic state which overwhelmed and placed in abeyance the personality of the recipient, who then became a passive mouthpiece for the god. Virgil provides a vivid description of the physical transformation wrought by divine inspiration in his portrayal of Aeneas' visit to the Sibyl. After Apollo had taken possession of the prophetess, Virgil relates,

> suddenly her countenance and her colour changed and her hair fell in disarray. Her breast heaved and her bursting heart was wild and mad; she appeared taller and spoke in no mortal tones, for the god was nearer and the breath of his power was upon her.[4]

Of great importance for the development of subsequent conceptions of inspiration was Plato, who devoted his attention to inspiration in several of his dialogues. In the *Phaedrus* he describes poetic inspiration as a 'kind of possession and madness' induced in the poet by the muses. Such madness is a sine qua non of poetic creation, Plato argues, commenting that

[3] See, for example, Homer, *Iliad*, Bk I, line 1; Hesiod, *Theogony*, lines 22–34; Pindar, *Paean*, VII B.
[4] Virgil, *Aeneid*, Bk. VI, lines 46–51; trans. W. F. Jackson Knight (Harmondsworth: Penguin, 1956).

> he who without the divine madness comes to the doors of the Muses, confident that he will be a good poet by art, meets with no success, and the poetry of the sane man vanishes into nothingness before that of the inspired madman.[5]

The most important and influential of Plato's treatments of inspiration, however, occurs in the *Ion*. In his speech on poetry,[6] Socrates speaks of how the muse or the god overrides the personality and rational faculties of the inspired individual, commenting that 'all the good epic poets utter all those fine poems not from art, but as inspired and possessed, and the good lyric poets likewise'.[7] Indeed, as the following passage makes clear, the divine extinguishing of the reason and personality of the poet is essential if we are to be sure that it is the god and not the poet who addresses us:

> And for this reason God takes away the mind of these men and uses them as his ministers, just as he does soothsayers and godly seers, in order that we who hear them may know that it is not they who utter these words of great price, when they are out of their wits, but that it is God himself who speaks and addresses us through them.[8]

[5] Plato, *Phaedrus*, 245 A; in *Plato*, vol. I, trans. Harold North Fowler (London: William Heinemann, 1914), pp. 412–579. For a discussion of Plato's conception of inspiration and its allegedly ironical nature, see E. N. Tigerstedt, *Plato's Idea of Poetical Inspiration* (Helsinki-Helsingfors: Commentationes Humanarum Litterarum, Societas Scientiarum Fennica, 1969).

[6] Plato, *Ion*, 533 D–534 E; in *Plato*, vol. III, trans. W. R. M. Lamb, (London: William Heinemann, 1925), pp. 406–47.

[7] Plato, *Ion*, 533 E; cf. Plato, *Laws*, 719 C, in *Plato*, vol. IX (London: William Heinemann, 1926).

[8] Plato, *Ion*, 534 C–D.

The poets are thus merely passive instruments of the gods. Divine communication is understood in terms of the god's dictation of his words to, or rather through, a passive human recipient who functions merely as a channel for conveying the divine message. The human being him or herself contributes nothing to the process other than providing the channel of communication between the god and human beings.

There are several passages in the Bible which seem to parallel the ancient Greek and Roman understanding of poetic creativity. The passages which lend the greatest biblical support to the instrumental conception of inspiration are those which describe God as speaking by the mouth of a chosen individual (Acts 1.16; 3.18; 4.25). Even more vivid are those texts which refer to God putting his words into the prophet's mouth. Thus Jeremiah describes his call as follows: 'Then the Lord put forth his hand and touched my mouth; and the Lord said to me, "Behold, I have put my words in your mouth"' (Jer 1.9; cf. Exod 4.15–16; Isa 59.21; Jer 15.19; Ezek 3.27; 11.5). Another vivid image for the mechanism of inspiration is that of God or a representative of God giving a chosen individual a scroll to eat (Ezek 2.8–3.3; 4 Ezra 14.39–40; Rev 10.8–11; cf. Jer 15.16).

Further parallels with Greek conceptions of inspiration seem to be present in biblical accounts of individuals having dramatic and extraordinary experiences as a result of the descent of the Spirit upon them. Thus we read of individuals falling into a prophetic rapture on receipt of the Spirit (Num 11.25; 1 Sam 10.6; 19.20–24; 1 Kgs 18.12; 2 Kgs 2.16; Ezek 3.12, 14; 8.3); having visions (Gen 15.1; 1 Kgs 22.19–22; Job 33.15–16; Jer 23. 18, 22; Ezek 8.3; 11.24; 40.2; 43.5); falling into a trance (Dan 10.9; Acts 10.10); and having what appear to be out-of-body experiences (Ezek 3.12, 14; 8.3; 11.1, 24; 37.1; 40.1; 43.5). Such passages seem to resemble Greek conceptions of inspiration, where the personality of the inspired individual is overwhelmed as the god takes possession of the individual and employs him or her as a passive mouthpiece.

The Platonic conception of poetic inspiration exerted considerable influence on the thinking of the Church Fathers.[9] Such a view of inspiration seems to lie behind the musical images employed by many Church Fathers, who frequently compare divine inspiration to a musician playing a musical instrument.[10] Augustine seems to adopt an instrumental understanding of inspiration when he writes that Christ made use of the biblical writers as if they were his own hands.[11] A different image is employed by Gregory the Great, who likens the inspired writer to a pen in God's hand.[12]

Many of the Fathers follow Plato in arguing that the human personality of the divinely inspired individual is

[9] For a discussion of instrumental conceptions of inspiration in the Fathers, see Luis Alonso Schökel, *The Inspired Word: Scripture in the Light of Language and Literature*, trans. by Francis Martin (London: Burns & Oates, 1967), pp. 58–66. Instrumental conceptions of inspiration can also be found in Hellenistic Judaism. See Philo, *Quis rerum divinarum heres*, 259; Josephus, *Antiquities* IV.6.5 (119, 121).

[10] Pseudo-Justin compares the biblical author to a harp or lyre played by the 'plectrum' that is the Divine Spirit (Justin, *Coh. ad Gr.* 8; PG 6:256). Similarly, Athenagoras portrays God's inspiration of the prophet as being like that of a flautist playing the flute (Athenagoras, *Legatio pro Christianis* 9; PG 6:905–7; cf. ch. 7; PG 6: 903–4), while Hippolytus prefers to describe the inspired biblical writer as a plectrum employed by the Holy Spirit (Hippolytus, *De Christo et Antichristo* 2; PG 10:729). John Chrysostom speaks of the Spirit playing St John and St Paul as if they were musical instruments (Chrysostom, *In Ioh. hom.*1, 2; *De Lazaro Concio.* 6, 9; PG 48:1041).

[11] Augustine, *De consens. evang.*, I.35.54.

[12] Gregory, *Morals on the Book of Job*, Preface I. 2.

extinguished for the duration of the inspiration. Athenagoras holds that the prophets prophesied κατ'ἔκωτασιν[13] and Ambrose speaks of the turbulence of the prophetic mind when in a state of inspiration.[14] Montanism also placed great weight on the ecstatic communication of divine revelation. Montanus, as well as his associates Priscilla and Maximilla, apparently lost consciousness during their reception and communication of the prophecies they allegedly received from the Holy Spirit. After joining the Montanists, Tertullian, too, adopted the instrumental conception of inspiration, writing that 'when a man is in the Spirit, especially when he has sight of the glory of God, or when God is speaking by him, he must of necessity fall out of his sense, because in fact he is overshadowed by the power of God.'[15]

The struggle of the Church with Montanism led to the ecstatic conception of inspiration being viewed with increasing suspicion. Indeed, as a result of the Montanist crisis, ecstasy became regarded as a mark of false prophecy and was no longer employed to categorize the inspiration of the biblical writers. Thus Epiphanius draws a clear distinction between the inspiration of the biblical authors and that of the Montanists. In contrast to the Montanists, the inspired writers of the Bible did not lose consciousness but comprehended the divine message imparted to them.[16] As a consequence of the Church's opposition to Montanism, the conception of the biblical writer as an impersonal, passive instrument gradually gave way to conceptions

[13] Athenagoras, *Legatio pro Christianis*, 9. A similar view can be found in Hellenistic Judaism. See Philo, *Quis rerum divinarum heres*. 249–66; *De spec. leg*. 4, 48f.

[14] Ambrose, *De Abrah*. 2, 61.

[15] Tertullian, *Adversus Marcionem*, ed. and trans. Ernest Evans (Oxford: Clarendon, 1972), IV, 22; cf. V, 8; *De Anima* XI, XXI.

[16] Epiphanius, *Haer*. 48, 1–10 (PG 41:855–71).

which placed greater weight on the involvement of the personality of the inspired writer. Thus although Hippolytus could speak of the biblical writer as a plectrum employed by the Holy Spirit, he could also at the same time conceive of inspiration in terms which left room for human participation in the composition of scripture. In *De Christo et Antichristo* 2 he speaks of inspiration not as overwhelming but as clarifying the mind of the inspired writer. A similar position is to be found in Origen, who distinguishes biblical from pagan inspiration on the grounds that, in contrast to pagan authors, the minds of the biblical writers were not extinguished by the Spirit but were enabled to grasp divine truth with greater clarity.[17]

The scholastic theory of inspiration can be regarded as a sophisticated version of the instrumental theories of inspiration developed in the early Church.[18] In many respects the theologians of the Middle Ages merely consolidated and systematized lines of thought already laid down in the patristic period. It is in this systematizing tendency that its significance lies, for it is in the scholastic period that a comprehensive doctrine of inspiration is at last developed. Indeed, according to Bruce Vawter,

> what emerged from the scholastic synthesis was the *only* theology of inspiration that has appeared in the entire history of the Church. Before it, existed only tentative thoughts, determinative of the directions taken by scholasticism but lacking the consistency necessary for a theology. After it, Christian thinking

[17] Origen, *C. Cels.* 7, 3–4; *In Ezech.* 6, 1 (PG 13:79).

[18] For an account of what he terms the 'scholastic synthesis' see Bruce Vawter, *Biblical Inspiration* (London: Hutchinson, 1972), ch. 3: 'The scholastic synthesis: Instrumental causality'. For Thomas Aquinas' conception of prophetic inspiration, see his *De Prophetia* in *Summa theologiae* 2a2ae, 171–4.

> has succeeded only in reacting in one way or another to the scholastic synthesis; it has never succeeded in replacing it.[19]

The scholastic theology of inspiration arises from the fusion of the model of inspiration inherited from the Fathers with Aristotelianism. Of particular importance in the development of the theory of inspiration was Aristotle's distinction between principal efficient cause and instrumental efficient cause. These two types of cause are best made clear by means of the example of someone writing with a piece of chalk.[20] The chalk is the instrumental efficient cause. It is on the basis of its qualities as a piece of chalk that the writing is able to take place. It is the *instrumental* efficient cause because it is the instrument by means of which the writing is caused. It does not of itself, however, cause the writing, because a piece of chalk does not possess the faculties of speech and thought that underlie the act of writing. The person holding the chalk is the principal efficient cause, directing the chalk in such a way that writing takes place. That is, the human being is the *principal* efficient cause, because it is he or she who intends the writing and makes use of the piece of chalk as the means for carrying it out. Moreover, the human being, as the principal efficient cause, extends the chalk beyond what the chalk is capable of achieving on its own. Yet the qualities of the chalk have been essential in allowing the human being to write.

This distinction between principal efficient cause and instrumental efficient cause was applied by the medieval theologians to the question of inspiration. The inspired individual is understood to be like our piece of chalk in that

[19] Vawter, ibid., p. 44 (original emphasis).
[20] Ibid., p. 48.

he or she is the instrument that makes divine communication possible. This does not mean, however, that the inspired individual is a lifeless tool in God's hands, for it is precisely his or her human qualities of thought and language that make it possible for God to make use of the individual. God, as the originator of the message to be communicated and as the power directing the human being in the communication of this message, is the principal efficient cause. It is he who makes use of the human qualities of the inspired individual in order to communicate his message. The message is thus God's – it is the Word of God – for it originates with him; yet it is also the inspired individual's word, for it has been possible to communicate it only by making use of the individual's human qualities. Furthermore, just as the piece of chalk was employed to carry out a task that went beyond its ability to achieve on its own, so too is the inspired individual 'used' by God in a way that goes beyond the normal human powers of that individual.

By emphasizing that it is the human qualities such as thought and language that enable God to make use of the inspired individual for the communication of his will, the scholastic model seems to leave more room for a human contribution to inspiration than patristic instrumental theories. Nevertheless, it ultimately suffers from the same problem, namely that unless clearer indication can be given as to how the human mind retains its autonomy under divine inspiration, the scholastic model implies the extinction of the personality of the inspired individual. The analogy of the chalk works because the chalk does not possess a mind and will. The problem with the analogy is its inability to indicate how God can employ the inspired individual in a way which does not reduce him or her to the level of a passive, inanimate object like a piece of chalk.

The dictation theory of inspiration

Closely related to the instrumental theory of inspiration is the 'dictation' theory, which holds that God dictated his message to the biblical writers in much the same way that someone might dictate a letter to a secretary or into a dictaphone. There are several passages in the Bible which seem to support this view of biblical inspiration. Thus Isaiah writes, 'Then the Lord said to me, "Take a large tablet and write upon it in common characters, 'Belonging to Maher-shalal-hash-baz'"' (Isa 8.1; cf. 8.11). Old Testament prophets can also be described as 'hearing' God's words (Isa 5.9; 22.14; Ezek 9.1), sometimes as a result of witnessing deliberations in the heavenly court (Ezek 9.3–8). There are also passages in the Old Testament which describe God as speaking *through* a chosen individual, which are compatible with both instrumental and dictation theories of inspiration (Num 36.13; Hag 1.1; Zech 7.7).

The dictation model of inspiration had its supporters in the early Church. Jerome, Chrysostom and Augustine could all occasionally speak of inspiration in terms of dictation.[21] Calvin, too, speaks of the dictation of scripture by the Spirit.[22] Dictation was also the dominant understanding of inspiration in the Protestant orthodoxy of the seventeenth century.[23] Quenstedt, for example, claims that

> The Holy Spirit not only inspired in the prophets and

[21] Jerome, *Letters* 120.10; Chrysostom, *In Illud, Salutate Priscillam et Aquilam (Rom. 16.3), et quae sequunter, sermo 1* (PG 51:187); Augustine, *De consens. evang.* I. 35.54.

[22] Calvin, *Institutes* IV. 8. 6 (OT), 8 (NT).

[23] For a study of seventeenth-century Protestant conceptions of inspiration, see J. K. S. Reid, *The Authority of Scripture*; Robert Preus, *The Inspiration of Scripture: A Study of the Theology of the Seventeenth Century Lutheran Dogmaticians* (Edinburgh: Oliver and Boyd, 1957).

> apostles the content and sense contained in Scripture, or the meaning of the words, so that they might of their own free will clothe and furnish these thoughts with their own style and words, but the Holy Spirit actually supplied, inspired and dictated the very words and each and every term individually.[24]

The dictation theory, however, suffers from the same problems as the instrumental theory. Neither seems able to do justice to the diversity and variety of the literature of the Bible. If God had really employed the inspired individual as a passive instrument and dictated the Bible verbatim to the biblical writers, we would arguably expect complete uniformity of style. This, however, as even a cursory reading of the Bible will reveal, is far from being the case. On the contrary, the Bible contains a variety of different styles of writing and different forms of literature. O'Collins asks:

> Did the Holy Spirit's style change from the decades when Paul's letters were written to the later period when the Gospels were composed? If the human authors played no real part in the literary process, such differences could only be due to a mysterious or even arbitrary divine choice to vary the style and alter the form.[25]

[24] Quenstedt, *Theol. did. pol.*, I. 72; quoted in Reid, *Authority of Scripture*, p. 85. See also Johannes Musaeus, *Introductio in theologiam* (Jena, 1679), theses 3–9 and 17 in the chapter entitled 'De natura et quidditate scripturae sacrae', pp. 245 ff.; in Emanuel Hirsch (ed.), *Hilfsbuch zum Studium der Dogmatik: Die Dogmatik der Reformatoren und der altevangelischen Lehrer quellenmäßig belegt und verdeutlicht* (Berlin and Leipzig: Walter de Gruyter, 1937, 1951), § 504, pp. 314–15.

[25] Gerald O'Collins, SJ, *Fundamental Theology* (London: Darton, Longman & Todd, 1981), 231.

Perhaps the most significant criticism of instrumental and dictation theories of inspiration, however, is that both theories seem to reduce the human being to a mere puppet. Leaving aside the question of the morality of such treatment of human beings, such a view of inspiration fails to do justice to the temperament and personality of the biblical writers, which is clearly discernible in many of the biblical texts. Although, as we have seen, there are passages which seem to support instrumental and dictation theories of inspiration, these must be tempered by the numerous texts in which the individuality and personality of the prophet are clearly evident. The biblical descriptions of the commissioning of Moses (Exod 3.1–4.17), Jeremiah (Jer 1.4–10), and Ananias (Acts 9.10–19), for example, are not of an overwhelming and overriding of the personality of the divinely chosen individual. On the contrary, Moses, Jeremiah and Ananias all argue with God, and initially even go so far as to resist the demands God makes of them. Indeed, God and, in the case of Ananias, the Risen Christ have to resort to persuasion in order to convince them to respond to the divine commission they have received. Furthermore, in 1 Peter the prophets are described as being conscious and creative participants in the formulation and communication of the divine message (1 Pet 1.10–12). The picture that emerges from the biblical accounts of God's calling of selected individuals is that of a living relationship between the divine and the human in which the individuality, personality, and autonomy of the human being is respected. The humanity of the divinely commissioned individual is not destroyed by the Spirit but freely works together with the Spirit.[26]

[26] This raises the question of the relationship between those passages in the Bible which seem to support instrumental and dictation theories of biblical inspiration and those texts which seem

If the dictation theory of inspiration is to be retained, it can only be in a qualified form which respects human autonomy and does not insist that every individual word in the Bible is due to divine dictation. Such a qualified version of dictation is proposed by Alonso Schökel, who argues that the relationship between God and the inspired individual is best understood as akin to that between an executive and a trusted and dependable secretary, to whom the executive gives responsibility for formulating in detail his broad outline of his policy. 'In these cases,' Alonso Schökel writes,

> there is a close collaboration, a union of mind and will, in order to produce the end result. The executive gives the general theme, sketches its development and some of its leading ideas, and perhaps proposes one or two good phrases which ought to be incorporated. The secretary draws up the document, which is then corrected and written once again in its final form.[27]

If we adopt this understanding of dictation, we are increasingly moving away from the view that inspiration resides in the individual words of the Bible and situating it rather in the general message or theme which those words convey. However, if we wish to continue to work with the dictation model of inspiration, Alonso Schökel's version of it may point the way forward.

to indicate a high degree of human participation in the composition of the biblical writings. One possible way of resolving the apparent conflict between such passages is to attribute instrumental conceptions of inspiration to a more primitive strand of Israel's religious thinking, which was then increasingly displaced by the development of a conception of inspiration as divine–human cooperation. There may be a hint of such a development in Jeremiah's distinction between the (false) prophet who prophesies on the basis of a dream and the (true) prophet who has God's Word and speaks it faithfully (Jer 23.25–28).

[27] Alonso Schökel, *Inspired Word*, pp. 71–2.

The theory of verbal inspiration

Adherents of the verbal inspiration theory hold that the very words of the Bible are inspired. That is, God does not merely inspire the biblical writers or their message but has inspired the choice of the words they employ. Such a view can be found in Irenaeus[28] and Clement of Alexandria; the latter, commenting on 2 Tim 3.15, claims that 'the letters which make us sacred and divine are themselves sacred, and the writings composed from these sacred letters and syllables, namely, the collected Scriptures, are consequently called by the same apostle "inspired of God"'[29] Hints of a conception of verbal inspiration can also be found in Origen and Jerome, though neither has any difficulty in holding a doctrine of verbal inspiration in conjunction with a conception of the gradation of scripture.[30]

The theory of verbal inspiration came into its own in the era of Protestant orthodoxy. In his *Clavis Scripturae Sacrae* Matthias Flacius went so far as to attribute the Hebrew pointing of the Old Testament to the activity of the Holy Spirit, commenting that, 'If the churches allow the devil to posit this theory [of the belated addition of the Hebrew vowels], then will not the entire scripture as such become uncertain for us?'[31] The theory of verbal inspiration

[28] Irenaeus, *Adv. Haer.* III, 16, 2; cf. II, 28, 2.

[29] Clement of Alexandria, *Protr.* IX, 82, 1; in *The Exhortation to the Greeks, The Rich Man's Salvation, and the Fragment of an Address Entitled to the Newly Baptized*, trans. G. W. Butterworth (Cambridge, MA: Harvard University Press, 1968).

[30] Origen, *Comm. in Psalm.* (PG 12: 1081); Jerome, *Comm. in ep. ad Eph.* I, 1, 8 (PG 26: 481).

[31] Matthias Flacius Illyricus, *Clavis Scripturae Sacrae*, vol. II, 8. 62. 646f., in Hirsch (ed.), *Hilfsbuch zum Studium der Dogmatik*, § 503, p. 314. This was a view taken up by Johann Buxtorf and subsequently made the official doctrine of the Swiss Reformed Church in the Formula Consensus Helvetica of 1675: Wolf-Dieter Hauschild, *Lehrbuch der Kirchen- und Dogmengeschichte*, 2 vols

received its first developed exposition, however, at the hands of Johann Gerhard, who argued that it is not merely the contents of the Bible that are inspired but the very words in which these contents are expressed.[32] Wilhelm Amesius makes a similar point when he writes that the Holy Spirit

> not only inspired the subject matter [of the supernatural revelation contained in scripture] but also dictated and supplied the individual words in which the subject matter was written down, which nevertheless occurred with such gentle accommodation that each writer made use of those modes of speech which were most appropriate to his person and situation.[33]

More recently, verbal inspiration has been defended by the Princeton School, the foremost representative of which was B. B. Warfield, who provides the following succinct and clear definition of verbal inspiration:

> The Church . . . has held from the beginning that the Bible is the Word of God in such a sense that its words, though written by men and bearing indelibly impressed upon them the marks of their human origin, were written, nevertheless, under such an influence of the Holy Ghost as to be also the words of God, the adequate expression of His mind and will. It has always recognized that this conception of co-authorship implies that the Spirit's superintendence

(Gütersloh: Chr. Kaiser/Gütersloher Verlagshaus, 1999–2000), II, p.

[32] Hauschild, ibid.

[33] Wilhelm Amesius, *Medulla theologica* (1659), I. 34, p. 151, in Hirsch (ed.), *Hilfsbuch zum Studium der Dogmatik*, § 643, p. 396.

> extends to the choice of the words by the human authors (verbal inspiration), and preserves its product from everything inconsistent with a divine authorship – thus securing, among other things, that entire truthfulness which is everywhere presupposed in and asserted for Scripture by the Biblical writers (inerrancy).[34]

At first sight this might appear to be very similar to the theory of dictation. However, supporters of verbal inspiration stress that God does not dictate his message *directly* to the prophets or apostles, but rather creates the conditions in which the biblical writers can receive and express the divine communication in the language which God finds most appropriate. God creates these conditions by guiding and influencing the circumstances into which the biblical writer is born, such as family, culture, occupation, education, etc., and by directing the writer's life in such a way that when the divine message is communicated to him he expresses it in precisely the words which God wishes to be employed. Consequently, not only is the conceptual content of the text inspired, but also the very words in which it is expressed.

The theory of verbal inspiration arose in an age when specific, named individuals were believed to have been responsible for the composition of the biblical texts. It is the names of these chosen individuals which are attached to the various writings of the Bible. Literary and historical analysis has revealed, however, that many of the biblical texts are not the result of the literary activity of one individual but came into existence over a long period of

[34] Benjamin Breckinridge Warfield, *The Inspiration and Authority of the Bible*, ed. Samuel Craig (Philadelphia: Presbyterian and Reformed Publishing Company, 1970), p. 173.

time and as the result of the agency of many, unnamed individuals. This has become particularly apparent in certain of the Old Testament writings, which were often the result of the bringing together and editing of a variety of different sources. This presents the theory of verbal inspiration with a serious problem: if the principle of personal authorship has been undermined in this way, how can we continue to speak of verbal inspiration? One way of dealing with this problem is to extend the concept of inspiration to all those involved in the composition of a biblical writing. All of the various contributors can then be regarded as 'inspired' authors. Another way of dealing with this problem is to attribute inspired status to the individual responsible for the *final* form of a biblical text. The literary sources upon which the author may have drawn, it is argued, are of no significance as far as the inspiration of the final text is concerned.

There are, however, serious problems with such attempts to adjust the theory of verbal inspiration. Biblical scholarship has revealed that in most cases the prophets were not themselves responsible for the final version of the texts that ultimately emerged bearing their names. Rather, the process seems to have been that the teaching of the prophets was handed down in oral form by their followers. In the process these oral traditions were modified and edited, before eventually being put into written form many years later. If we argue that inspiration resides in the final version of a text, we are in the odd position of regarding the final edition of a prophetic work as more inspired than the prophet whose utterances ultimately led to the composition of the work.

Perhaps the greatest weakness of the theory of verbal inspiration, however, is that in its traditional form it commits us to the doctrine of biblical inerrancy, for if God is responsible for the very words employed by the inspired writer, then it is inconceivable that the Bible could contain any error. As we shall see later, this theory is undermined by the insuperable difficulties facing the doctrine of biblical inerrancy.

The theory of plenary inspiration

The existence of errors and inconsistencies in the Bible has led some scholars to limit inspiration to certain areas of scripture, a view which is often described as the theory of the gradation of scripture.[35] Passages of no doctrinal or spiritual significance, which are often the passages that contain historical inaccuracies, need not be regarded as inspired or can be regarded as less inspired than other, more 'spiritual' passages of scripture. This approach has been resisted by both Catholics and Protestants alike, who have argued that if inspiration is to mean anything it must be applied to the whole of the Bible. If this is not the case, the argument goes, then it is difficult to know where to draw the line between inspired, non-inspired and less inspired parts of the Bible. The understanding of inspiration which emphasizes that the *whole* of the Bible is inspired is known as 'plenary' inspiration.

The theory of plenary inspiration has been advocated by both Catholic and Protestant theologians. It was affirmed at the Council of Trent, which, after listing the works it regarded as canonical, threatened with anathema all those who failed to acknowledge these works 'in their entirety and with all their parts',[36] a view which was reaffirmed at

[35] See Vawter, *Biblical Inspiration*, pp. 65–8, 134–6, for a survey of theories of gradation of scripture.
[36] H. J. Schroeder (ed.), *Canons and Decrees of the Council of Trent* (St Louis, MO: B. Herder, 1941), p. 18.

the First Vatican Council.[37] It has also been vigorously defended by Evangelical scholars such as Warfield, who defines plenary inspiration as

> the doctrine that the Bible is inspired not *in part* but *fully*, in all its elements alike, – things discoverable by reason as well as mysteries, matters of history and science as well as of faith and practice, words as well as thoughts.[38]

An even more succinct definition of the theory is provided by the Swiss Evangelical scholar René Pache, who writes that the expression 'plenary inspiration' 'signifies that the inspiration is entire and without restriction'.[39] It is the plenary inspiration of the Bible, Warfield tells us, that has been 'the assured persuasion of the people of God from the first planting of the church until today'.[40]

Examination of the concept of plenary inspiration reveals that it is made up of two distinct claims. The first claim is that *all* of scripture is inspired. The second claim is that the various biblical writings are all inspired *in the same way*. There can be no gradations of inspiration or restriction of inspiration to those passages which meet with modern approval. To these two claims is usually added a third, namely that plenary inspiration commits us to a doctrine of *verbal* inspiration.

[37] For a discussion of the understanding of inspiration affirmed at the First Vatican Council, see Johannes Beumer, *Die katholische Inspirationslehre zwischen Vatikanum I und II: Kirchliche Dokumente im Licht der theologischen Diskussion* (Stuttgart: Katholisches Bibelwerk, 1967), pp. 11–20.

[38] Warfield, *Inspiration and Authority of the Bible*, p. 113 (original emphasis).

[39] René Pache, *The Inspiration and Authority of Scripture*, trans. by Helen I. Needham (Chicago: Moody Press, 1969), p. 72.

[40] Warfield, *Inspiration and Authority of the Bible*, p. 106.

There is certainly evidence that the Church Fathers subscribed to the theory of plenary inspiration in the first sense, namely that all of scripture is inspired. Thus Irenaeus sees the Bible as 'spiritual in its entirety'.[41] Gregory of Nyssa interprets 2 Tim 3.16 to mean that all scripture is due to the Holy Spirit.[42] Origen and Gregory Nazianzus hold that the influence of the Holy Spirit extended down to the most insignificant details of the text.[43] Indeed, Origen even went so far as to detect the activity of the Holy Spirit in the grammatical and stylistic infelicities of scripture.[44] Similarly, Jerome claims that 'in the divine Scriptures every word, syllable, accent and point is packed with meaning'.[45] To those who doubted the spiritual significance of Paul's Letter to Philemon, Jerome responded that this indicated an inability to recognize the power and wisdom contained in the letter.[46] So convinced was Chrysostom that scripture contains nothing that is superfluous ('in Scriptura nihil superfluum') that he attributed spiritual significance to the chronologies and name lists of the Bible,[47] and even found himself able to write two homilies on the divine origin of the salutations in Romans 16.[48]

Modern supporters of plenary inspiration, however, base their defence first and foremost on the Bible, claiming that it contains a number of passages that support the theory. Pache, for example, claims that plenary inspiration 'is what

[41] Irenaeus, *Adv. Haer.* 2, 28, 2.
[42] Gregory of Nyssa, *C. Eunom.* 7 (PG 45: 744).
[43] Origen, *In ps.* 1, 4 (PG 12: 1081); *Hom. in Ierem.* 39, 1 (PG 13: 544, 545); Gregory Nazianzus, *Or.* 2, 105.
[44] Origen, *In Os.* (PG 13, 825–26).
[45] Jerome, *In Eph.* 2 (3, 6).
[46] Jerome, *In Philem.* prologue.
[47] Chrysostom, *In Illud, Vidi Dominum, hom.* 2, 2 (PG 56, 110).
[48] Chrysostom, *In Illud, Salutate Priscillam et Aquilam, (Rom. 16.3) et quae sequentur, Sermo 1* (PG 51: 187).

the sacred authors everywhere affirm',[49] and in support of this claim cites 2 Tim 3.16; 1 Thess 2.13; Rev 22.18–19; and Matt 5.18. But do these texts in fact support the claim that the Bible is inspired not only in its entirety but also in the same way? Do these passages imply that the Bible rejects the notion of a gradation of scripture?

The key text for supporters of plenary inspiration is 2 Tim 3.16. There are, however, problems in the translation and interpretation of this passage, owing to the ambiguity of the Greek.[50] One possible translation of the Greek phrase *πᾶσα γραφὴ* θεόπνευστος is '*All scripture that is inspired of God* is profitable for learning.' This reading, however, is consistent with a doctrine of the gradation of inspiration, for it can be read as implying that there are two types of scripture, namely that which is inspired by God and that which is not inspired by God. Only the former is profitable for learning.

The usual translation of 2 Tim 3.16 adopted by supporters of the theory of plenary inspiration, however, is, '*All scripture is inspired by God* and is profitable for learning.' This is taken to mean that the whole of the Bible is inspired in the same way. There are problems with this interpretation of 2 Tim 3.16, however. First, the passage seems to indicate merely that God is the originator of

[49] Pache, *Inspiration and Authority of Scripture*, p. 72.

[50] For discussions of the meaning of this passage, see J. N. D. Kelly, *A Commentary on the Pastoral Epistles* (London: Adam & Charles Black, 1963), pp. 202–4; Eduard Schweizer, *θεοπνευστος*, in Gerhard Kittel (ed.), *Theological Dictionary of the New Testament*, trans. and ed. Geoffrey W. Bromiley, 10 vols (Grand Rapids: Eerdmans, 1964–76), vol. VI, pp. 453–5. For evangelical discussions, see Warfield, *Inspiration and Authority of the Bible*, pp. 245–96; reprinted from *The Presbyterian and Reformed Review* 11 (1900), 89–130, 'God-inspired Scripture'; Paul D. Feinberg, 'The meaning of inerrancy', in Norman Geisler, *Inerrancy* (Grand Rapids: Zondervan 1979), pp. 265–304; 277–80.

scripture. It does not explicitly state that *every* aspect of scripture is inspired, down to the smallest detail. Secondly, the 'scripture' to which the author of 2 Timothy is almost certainly referring is the Septuagint version of the Old Testament rather than the whole of the Bible. At the time of the composition of 2 Timothy (probably early second century[51]) the canonization of the Christian Bible had not yet been brought to completion. Although a degree of consensus had been reached with regard to the Synoptic Gospels and ten of the Pauline letters, it would still be several centuries before our present New Testament would be accepted as 'scripture'.[52] At best, then, 2 Tim 3.16 can be read as affirming the inspired status of *part* of the Christian Bible. It thus seems unable to do the work that supporters of plenary inspiration require of it.

There are similar problems with the use of 1 Thess 2.13 to support plenary inspiration. Paul's claim that the Thessalonians have received the Word of God and not the word of men does not of itself contain the claim that the whole of the scriptures is inspired. It is, moreover, highly questionable whether the phrase 'word of God' used here applies to scripture. It is more likely that Paul is employing it as a periphrasis for the Gospel message. Furthermore, even if we accept that the phrase 'word of God' refers to scripture, Paul cannot have the whole of our present Bible in mind for the simple reason that the Gospels, the Acts of the Apostles, and the letters of Peter were – at least in their final scripturally authoritative form – not yet in existence.

Rev 22.18–19 also fails to do the work required of it by Pache. First, the threat the author of Revelation levels at

[51] W. G. Kümmel, *Introduction to the New Testament* (London: SCM Press, 1975), 387.

[52] See Hans von Campenhausen, *The Formation of the Christian Bible* (London: Adam & Charles Black, 1972); F. F. Bruce, *The Canon of Scripture* (Glasgow: Chapter House, 1988).

'anyone [who] takes away from the words of the book of this prophecy' refers only to the Apocalypse and makes no mention of the rest of the Bible. This passage can therefore be used in defence of plenary inspiration only by extending it beyond its literal, plain and obvious meaning, which is surely an illegitimate procedure for an Evangelical Christian! Secondly, the denial that the whole of the Bible is uniformly inspired need not be construed as 'a taking away from the words of scripture'. It could be argued that the organization of the biblical texts according to the gradation of scripture is a means of allowing the central message of the Bible to become more apparent. That is, the theory of the gradation of scripture need not be interpreted as a removal of the words of scripture and thus a violation of Rev 22.18–19, but as a means of subordinating less worthy and significant strands to those that are worthy and significant. Subordination is not synonymous with removal, consequently the theory of gradation of scripture is not incompatible with Rev 22.18–19.

Pache is on no stronger ground when he cites Matt 5.18 in support of the theory of plenary inspiration: 'For truly, I say to you, till heaven and earth pass away, not an iota, not a dot, will pass from the law until all is accomplished.' Certainly this text could be employed to support the claim that the *law* is fully inspired, but this is not sufficient to support a doctrine of the inspiration of *all* of scripture. Furthermore, it does not of itself undermine the theory of gradations of inspiration. It is possible to subscribe to the view that not a jot or tittle will pass from the law and simultaneously to argue that a hierarchy should be imposed upon this material. Indeed, it could be argued that this is the thrust of the antitheses that follow Matt 5.17–20.

A further argument that Pache advances in support of plenary inspiration is that scripture attaches great significance ‘to the exact reception and communication of the divine expressions’. In support of this claim he asserts that ‘Moses well knew that he was transmitting the very words of God in the book of the law, just as he did in the case of the tables of stone which contained the Ten Commandments.’[53] Among several passages that Pache cites as evidence for biblical emphasis on the exact transmission of the divine will are passages in which God is described as putting his words into an individual’s mouth,[54] as well as Matt 24.35 and Rev 19.9; 21.5; 22.6, all of which, he claims, stress the truthfulness and trustworthiness of God’s Word.

Once again, however, Pache is demanding of the texts more than they can deliver. He is certainly right in his claim that the passages he cites express their writers’ conviction that God’s word is true and trustworthy. It is something altogether different, however, to claim that this means that every aspect of the Bible is equally and ‘fully’ inspired, for there is nothing in the texts themselves to prevent us from reading them as references to the reliability of the message the individual receives rather than to the exact wording of a phrase God has allegedly put into the mouth of a chosen person. In other words, Pache’s evidence makes clear only that the various individuals mentioned in the passages he cites take their reception of the divine communication very seriously. It does not show, however, that we are committed to accepting that the texts which eventually emerged as a consequence of this divine communication are uniformly inspired in all their various aspects.

The biblical evidence, then, simply fails to support the theory of plenary inspiration. Of the three elements of the

[53] Pache, *Inspiration and Authority of Scripture*, p. 72.
[54] Num 22.38; 24.13; 2 Sam 23.2; Jer 1.9, 17; 23.28; 26.2; 36.2; cf. Isa 51.16; Ezek 2.7–8; 3.10–11, 17; Deut 18.18.

theory – that all scripture is inspired, that all scripture is inspired in the same way, and that the very words of the Bible are inspired – only the first has some biblical support. Even here, however, the evidence is not sufficient to support the arguments of the advocates of plenary inspiration, for all that 2 Tim 3.16 says is that scripture ultimately owes its existence to God. It does *not* make the claim that all the material of every biblical writing is inspired. As we shall see later, there are more appropriate ways of treating the biblical material.

The inerrancy of the Bible

Besides situating biblical inspiration in the *words* of the Bible, the theories we have examined are united by their insistence on the inerrancy of scripture, a view which has been vigorously defended by Catholic and Evangelical Protestant thinkers alike.[55]

[55] It is frequently claimed by its supporters that biblical inerrancy is the historic teaching of the Church. See 'Chicago Statement on Biblical Inerrancy', Article XVI: for text and exposition, see Carl F. H. Henry, *God, Revelation and Authority*, 6 vols (Waco, TX: Word Books, 1976–83), vol. 4, pp. 211–19; ibid., vol. IV, § 16; 'The view of the Bible held by the Church: The Early Church through Luther', in Geisler (ed.), *Inerrancy*, pp. 355–82; John H. Gerstner, 'The Church's doctrine of biblical inspiration', in James Montgomery Boice (ed.), *The Foundation of Biblical Authority* (Grand Rapids: Zondervan, 1978), pp. 23–58; 'The view of the Bible held by the Church: Calvin and the Westminster Divines', in Geisler (ed.), *Inerrancy*, pp. 383–410; Jacob A. O. Preus, *It is Written* (St Louis: Concordia, 1971), pp. 43–72; Richard Lovelace, 'Inerrancy: Some historical perspectives', in Roger Nicole and J. Ramsey Michaels (eds), *Inerrancy and Common Sense* (Grand Rapids: Baker Book House, 1980), pp. 15–47; esp. pp. 20–26; Harold Lindsell, *The Battle for the Bible* (Grand Rapids: Zondervan, 1976), pp. 42–43. For a critique of this view, see Jack B. Rogers, 'The church doctrine of biblical authority', in Donald K. McKim (ed.), *The Authoritative Word: Essays on the Nature of*

Catholic views of inerrancy

The Catholic adherence to biblical inerrancy stems from the concept of the divine authorship of scripture. Put in its most simple form, the Catholic position is that if God is the ultimate author of scripture, then whatever is in scripture must be true.[56] In the encyclical *Providentissimus Deus*, issued on 18 November 1893, Pope Leo XIII makes explicit this connection between divine authorship and the inerrancy of scripture:

> By a supernatural power [God] so instigated and moved [the inspired writers] to the task of writing, and so assisted them while writing, that all those things and only those things which he commanded they rightly conceived in their minds, faithfully willed to write down, and aptly expressed with infallible truth; otherwise he would not be the author of the whole sacred Scripture.[57]

Fifty years later Pius XII advanced a more differentiated conception of inerrancy to accommodate the insights of biblical criticism and awareness of the diversity of literary forms in the Bible. The encyclical *Divino Afflante Spiritu* (1943) states:

> For . . . in many cases in which the sacred authors are accused of some historical inaccuracy or of the inexact

Scripture (Grand Rapids: Eerdmans, 1983), pp. 197–224.

[56] For a survey of Catholic works on biblical inspiration and inerrancy, see Alonso Schökel, *Inspired Word*; James Tunstead Burtchaell, *Catholic Theories of Biblical Inspiration since 1810: A Review and Critique* (Cambridge: Cambridge University Press, 1969).

[57] Quoted in Vawter, *Biblical Inspiration*, p. 72.

> recording of some events, it is found to be a question of nothing more than those customary and characteristic forms of expression or styles of narrative which were current in human intercourse among the ancients, and which were in fact quite legitimately and commonly employed.[58]

Despite this concession to biblical scholarship, however, the Catholic position remained the assertion that because God is the author of scripture, scripture must be free of error: 'For just as the substantial Word of God becomes like to men in all things, "without sin", so the words of God, expressed in human language, became in all things like to human speech except error.'[59]

The Second Vatican Council, however, moved away from the strict inerrancy of previous papal pronouncements.[60] In the third chapter of the Dogmatic Constitution on Divine Revelation entitled 'The divine inspiration and the interpretation of sacred Scripture',[61] it is declared that the books of the Old and New Testament are in their totality 'sacred and canonical, because having been written under the inspiration of the Holy Spirit ('Spiritu sancto inspirante

[58] Pius XII, *Encyclical Letter: Divino Afflante Spiritu*, trans. G. D. Smith (London: Catholic Truth Society, 1944), § 42, p. 26.
[59] Ibid., § 41, p. 26.
[60] For developments in Catholic thinking on inspiration between the two Vatican Councils, see Beumer, *Die katholische Inspirationslehre zwischen Vatikanum I und II*.
[61] English translation in Walter M. Abbott (ed.), *The Documents of Vatican II* (London: Geoffrey Chapman, 1967), Dogmatic Constitution on Divine Revelation, pp. 111–32; ch. 3, pp. 118–121. For studies of the doctrine of inspiration espoused at Vatican II, see Otto Semmelroth and Maximilian Zerwick, *Vatikanum II über das Wort Gottes* (Stuttgart: Katholisches Bibelwerk, 1966), esp. pp. 28–39; Alois Grillmeier, in H. Vorgrimler (ed.), *Commentary on the Documents of Vatican II*, 5 vols (London: Burns & Oates, 1967–9), vol. 3, pp. 199–246, esp. pp. 231–7.

conscripti') . . . they have God as their author and have been handed on as such to the Church herself.' The consequence of the divine origin of scripture is that the Bible is free of error:

> Since everything asserted by the inspired authors or sacred writers must be held to be asserted by the Holy Spirit, it follows that the books of Scripture must be acknowledged as teaching firmly, faithfully, and without error that truth which God wanted put into the sacred writings for the sake of our salvation.[62]

What is interesting here is that although emphasis continues to be placed on the inerrancy of scripture, the last phrase of the passage seems to indicate a limitation of inerrancy to matters essential for faith. It is thus implied that the Bible may contain problematic material, but that, since it has no bearing on God's plan of salvation, this material is of no significance. Vatican II, then, seems to have shifted from the strict inerrancy of Vatican I to a conception of the limited inerrancy of scripture.[63]

Protestant views of biblical inerrancy

The question of biblical inerrancy has been particularly acute in Protestant theology and a vast literature has accumulated on the subject. This concern with inerrancy is a consequence of the Protestant doctrine of *sola scriptura* and the concomitant rejection of the Catholic doctrines of tradition and ecclesial authority. Since for Protestantism the only legitimate foundation for theology

[62] Abbott (ed.), *Documents of Vatican II*, p. 119.

[63] For an account of the discussions which led to this shift, see Vawter, *Biblical Inspiration*, pp. 143–50.

is the Bible, this foundation had to be made absolutely secure, something which was felt to be possible only by affirming the status of the Bible as the inerrant expression of the divine will.

As a result of their adherence to the doctrine of verbal inspiration, several theologians in the era of Protestant orthodoxy (1600–1750) affirmed the inerrancy of the Bible, namely Johann Gerhard,[64] Johann Quenstedt,[65] Francis Turrettin,[66] Johannes Musaeus,[67] and David Hollaz.[68] Of particular interest for modern discussion of inerrancy are the Swiss Calvinist theologian Louis Gaussen[69] and the nineteenth century Reformed theologians of Princeton Seminary, namely Archibald Alexander,[70] Charles Hodge,[71] Archibald Alexander Hodge[72] and Benjamin

[64] Johann Gerhard, *Loci theologici* (1610–22).

[65] Johann Quenstedt, *Theologia didactico-polemica sive systema theologicum* (1657).

[66] Franciscus Turrettinus, *Institutio Theologiae Elencticae*, 3 vols (Geneva, 1680–1685), I, 2.

[67] Johannes Musaeus, *Introductio in theologiam*, 539–540; in Hirsch (ed.), *Hilfsbuch zum Studium der Dogmatik*, § 505, p. 316.

[68] David Hollaz, *Examen theologicum acroamaticum* (1725), I. 67; in Hirsch (ed.), *Hilfsbuch zum Studium der Dogmatik*, § 492, p. 310.

[69] L. Gaussen, *The Divine Inspiration of the Bible*, trans. David D. Scott (Grand Rapids: Kregel, 1971).

[70] Archibald Alexander, *Evidences of the Authenticity, Inspiration, and Canonical Authority of the Holy Scriptures* (Philadelphia: Presbyterian Board of Publication, 1836).

[71] Charles Hodge, *Systematic Theology*, 3 vols (New York: Scribner's, 1899; reprinted London: James Clarke, 1960), vol. 1, pp. 151–88.

[72] Archibald Alexander Hodge and Benjamin Breckinridge Warfield, 'Inspiration', *The Presbyterian Review*, 2 (April 1881); reprinted with introduction and appendices by Roger R. Nicole as Archibald A. Hodge and Benjamin B. Warfield, *Inspiration* (Grand Rapids; Baker Book House, 1979). See also the chapter entitled 'The Inspiration of the Bible', in A. A. Hodge, *Outlines of Theology* (rev. edn 1879, reprinted, Grand Rapids: Zondervan, 1972), pp. 65–81; also A. A. Hodge, *Evangelical Theology* (Edinburgh: Banner of Truth Trust, 1979).

Breckinridge Warfield.[73] These Princeton theologians are particularly important because, in contrast to most of their predecessors, they were far more conscious of the impact of the rise of science and the development of historical-critical methods on the status of the Bible. The issue of inerrancy continues to be an important issue in contemporary Evangelicalism.[74]

A common argument in support of biblical inerrancy is based on the nature of God. God, it is held, cannot contradict himself, nor does he lie. Self-contradiction and mendacity are incompatible with God's omniscience and goodness. Consequently, since it is God who is ultimately the author of the Bible, it is inconceivable that God could permit errors of any kind to be incorporated into the Bible. As Quenstedt puts it, 'Whatever has been inspired by God is also trustworthy and above human criticism; it is at all

[73] Warfield, *Inspiration and Authority of the Bible*; see also *Limited Inspiration* (Philadelphia: Presbyterian and Reformed, no date).

[74] The literature on inerrancy is vast. The following is a representative but by no means exhaustive selection of supporters of biblical inerrancy: Edward J. Young, *Thy Word is Truth* (Grand Rapids: Eerdmans, 1957); Pache, *Inspiration and Authority of Scripture*, pp. 45–79, 120–58; John Warwick Montgomery (ed.), *God's Inerrant Word: An International Symposium on the Trustworthiness of Scripture* (Minneapolis: Bethany, 1974); Gleason L. Archer, 'The witness of the Bible to its own inerrancy', in Boice (ed.), *Foundation of Biblical Authority*, pp. 85–99; 'Alleged errors and discrepancies in the original manuscripts of the Bible', in Geisler, *Inerrancy*, pp. 55–82; Paul D. Feinberg, 'The Meaning of Inerrancy,' in Geisler (ed.), *Inerrancy*, pp. 267–304; Roger Nicole, 'The nature of inerrancy,' in Roger Nicole and J. Ramsey Michaels (eds), *Inerrancy and Common Sense* (Grand Rapids: Baker, 1980), pp. 71–95; James Packer, *'Fundamentalism' and the Word of God* (London: Inter-Varsity Press, 1958); Clark H. Pinnock, *Biblical Revelation – The Foundation of Christian Theology* (Chicago: Moody Press, 1971), esp. pp. 73–81; John Murray, 'The Attestation of Scripture', in Westminster Seminary, *The Infallible Word: A Symposium* (Phillipsburg, NJ: Presbyterian and Reformed Publishing Co., 1978), pp. 1–54.

times and under all circumstances true, free of all error and deceit.'[75]

Supporters of biblical inerrancy also point to the dire consequences of admitting that the Bible contains errors. If we concede that the Bible contains self-contradictions, inconsistencies and falsehoods, it is claimed, then we are faced by two intolerable conclusions. Either we are forced to conclude that since a particular text is erroneous it cannot have been inspired by the Holy Spirit; in which case we are confronted by the problem of which other passages are similarly lacking in divine inspiration. As John Wesley puts it, 'If there be any mistakes in the Bible, there may well be a thousand. If there be one falsehood in that book, it did not come from the God of truth.'[76] Or we are forced to concede that the Holy Spirit has inspired a text that contains an error, which raises the question of how many other areas of Christian belief have been due to errors on the part of the Holy Spirit. As Bahnsen puts it, 'After all, if God sets forth false assertions in minor areas where our research can check His accuracy (such as in historical or geographical details), how do we know that He does not also err in major concerns like theology?'[77] Both conclusions are, of course, unacceptable to the believer in biblical inerrancy. What the supporter of biblical inerrancy fears is the corrosive effect

[75] Quenstedt, *Theologia didactico-polemica*, I, 79; quoted in Robert Preus, *Inspiration of Scripture*, p. 86.

[76] John Wesley, *Journal*, Wednesday, July 24, 1776, in Nehemiah Curock (ed.), *The Journal of the Rev. John Wesley, A. M.*, 8 vols (London: Robert Culley (vol. 1), Charles H. Kelly (vols 2–8), 1909–16), vol. 6, p. 117; see also Lovelace, 'Inerrancy: Some historical perspectives,' in Nicole and Ramsey Michaels, *Inerrancy and Common Sense*, pp. 26–36.

[77] Greg L. Bahnsen, 'The inerrancy of the autographa', in Geisler, *Inerrancy*, pp. 149–93; 153. See Young, *Thy Word is Truth*, pp. 88–9; cf. Lovelace, 'Inerrancy: Some historical perspectives,' in Nicole and Ramsey Michaels, *Inerrancy and Common Sense*, p. 33.

of conceding the presence of a single error in the Bible on the Bible's claim to be the truth. If the Bible contains one error, why should it not contain many more, including errors concerning the fundamental doctrines of the faith?

The most important argument advanced by Evangelical scholars in support of the inerrancy of the Bible, however, is that the Bible itself claims to be inerrant. By far the most important text cited in support of this claim is 2 Tim. 3.16, a text which we have already encountered in another context. According to Gaussen, 2 Tim 3.16 indicates that the biblical writers believed that 'their writing is inspired, their narratives are directed from above; it is always God who speaks, who relates, who ordains or reveals by their mouth'.[78] From this Gaussen derives a doctrine of biblical inerrancy: 2 Tim 3.16 proves, he argues, that scripture cannot contain error of any kind. It proves that the Bible's own view of itself is that it is inerrant.

After 2 Tim 3.16 the most important passage for supporters of biblical inerrancy is 2 Pet 1.21: 'No prophecy ever came by the impulse of man, but men moved by the Holy Spirit spoke from God.' However, although this passage is often treated as a proof-text for a biblical doctrine of inspiration, it does not actually employ the term 'inspiration' in the Greek original. Furthermore, it speaks not of scripture but merely of 'prophecy'. Warfield deals with this latter problem by arguing that, since 'the entirety of scripture is elsewhere conceived of and spoken of as prophetic', the term 'prophecy' in 2 Peter can be read as standing for scripture as a whole.[79] Also important for Warfield's argument is the interpretation of the term *pheromenoi*, which the RSV translates as 'moved'. Warfield uses the Authorized Version, however, and this translation

[78] Gaussen, *Divine Inspiration of the Bible*, p. 25.
[79] Warfield, *Inspiration and Authority of the Bible*, pp. 135–6.

adopts the term 'borne', thus translating the verse as: 'no prophecy ever came by the will of man, but it was *borne* by the Holy Spirit'. This use of the term 'borne' is important, for Warfield bases his interpretation of the whole passage upon it. Warfield interprets 'borne' as follows: 'What is "borne" is taken up by the '"bearer", and conveyed by the bearer's power, not its own, to the bearer's goal, not its own.'[80] On the basis of this interpretation, Warfield claims that 2 Peter is making clear that God employs human beings as instruments for his message, but does so in a way which undermines neither their humanity nor the message they are given to impart.

In conjunction with 2 Tim 3.16 and 2 Pet 1.21, appeal is often made to John 14.26 and similar passages to support the claim that the Bible regards itself as inerrant. According to John 14.26 Jesus informed his disciples that, once he had departed, 'the Holy Spirit, whom the Father will send in my name . . . will teach you all things, and bring to your remembrance all that I have said to you'. That is, once Jesus is no longer with them, the disciples will be guided by the Holy Spirit. It is inconceivable, the argument then runs, that the Holy Spirit could have directed the disciples to write erroneously when some of their number later came to compose the New Testament. Consequently, the New Testament must be inerrant.

Another strategy often employed in support of biblical inerrancy is to appeal to Jesus' attitude to scripture. The New Testament records that Jesus frequently cited the Old Testament and clearly believed it to possess authority. The Son of God would not have made such frequent use of the Old Testament, it is argued by supporters of inerrancy, if he did not believe it to be the inerrant Word of God. Consequently, if Jesus understood the Old Testament in

[80] Ibid., p. 137.

this way, the argument runs, then we too, as followers of Jesus, should treat it in the same way.[81] This means treating the Old Testament and, by extension, the New Testament as the inerrant Word of God, since this, it is argued, is how the Old Testament was treated by Jesus himself. Supporters of this position frequently appeal to Matt 5.17–18 and John 10.35. The fact that Jesus speaks in Matthew 5 of not abolishing but fulfilling the law and that 'not an iota, not a dot, will pass from the law until all is accomplished' is taken by supporters of biblical inerrancy to mean that Christians are obliged to accept that the Old Testament is inerrant. In John 10.35, Jesus, after appealing to Ps 82.6 in justification of his claim that he sustains an intimate relation to the Father, states that 'scripture cannot be broken'. Warfield notes that Jesus prefaces his quotation of Psalm 82 by saying to the Jews: 'Is it not

[81] See A. M'Caig, *The Grand Old Book, being Lectures on Inspiration and Higher Criticism* (London: Elliot Stock, 1894); Edward John Carnell, *The Case for Orthodox Theology* (Philadelphia: Westminster, 1959), pp. 33–50; Clark Pinnock, 'The inspiration of Scripture and the authority of Jesus Christ', in John Warwick Montgomery (ed.), *God's Inerrant Word*, pp. 201–18; Robert Sproul, 'The case for inerrancy: A methodological analysis', in Montgomery (ed.), *God's Inerrant Word*, pp. 242–61; John Wenham, *Christ and the Bible* (London: Tyndale, 1972); 'Christ's view of Scripture', in Geisler (ed.), *Inerrancy*, pp. 3–36; John Gerstner, 'A Protestant view of biblical authority', in Frederick Greenspahn (ed.), *Scripture in the Jewish and Christian Traditions: Authority, Interpretation, Relevance* (Nashville: Abingdon, 1982), pp. 41–63. Pierre Ch. Marcel, 'Our Lord's use of Scripture', in Carl F. H. Henry (ed.), *Revelation and the Bible* (London: Tyndale, 1958), pp. 119–34; Roger Nicole, 'New Testament use of the Old Testament', in Henry (ed.), *Revelation and the Bible*, pp. 135–51; Edward J. Young, 'The authority of the Old Testament', in Westminster Seminary, *Infallible Word*, pp. 55–91, esp. 56–62; Jacob A. O. Preus, *It is Written*, pp. 11–42. This argument can be extended to the Apostles. See Edwin A. Blum, 'The Apostles' view of Scripture', in Geisler (ed.), *Inerrancy*, pp. 37–53; Jacob A. O. Preus, *It is Written*, pp. 43–72.

written in your *law*'.[82] That is, Jesus seems to regard the Psalms as part of the law and to attribute legal status to them, which he does, Warfield claims, not because of any legal content that the Psalms might have, 'but because it is a part of Scripture at large'.[83] What Jesus is saying in John 10.35 then, is that scripture has what Warfield terms 'indefectible authority'.[84] To put it in more conventional language, John 10.35 is another instance of the Bible claiming to be inerrant.

A further argument that the Bible claims inspired and inerrant status for itself is based on the New Testament's citation of passages from the Old Testament as if they had been spoken directly by God. In some New Testament passages quotations from the Old Testament are ascribed to 'scripture' which in the Old Testament original were uttered by God.[85] In other passages God[86] or the Holy Spirit[87] is described as having uttered passages quoted from the Old Testament. Commenting on such passages, Warfield writes:

> In one of these classes of passages the Scriptures are spoken of as if they were God; in the other, God is spoken of as if He were the Scriptures: in the two together, God and the Scriptures are brought into such conjunction as to show that in point of direct-

[82] John 10.34. Emphasis added.
[83] Warfield, *Inspiration and Authority of the Bible*, p. 138.
[84] Ibid., pp. 139–40.
[85] See, for example, Rom 9.17, where we find written not 'God says' but 'scripture says to Pharaoh, "I have raised you up . . ".'
[86] Examples can be found in Matt 15.4; Acts 3.25; 7.2–3, 6–7; 13. 47 (cf. 13.22); 2 Cor. 6.16–18; Heb. 1.5–8, 13; 5.5–6; 6.13–14; 7.21; 8.8; 10.30; 12.26; Jas 2.11.
[87] See, for example, Heb 3.7, where the quotation of Ps 95.7–11 is prefaced by the phrase 'Therefore, as the Holy Spirit says . . .' See also Acts 28.25; Heb 10.15.

> ness of authority no distinction was made between them.[88]

In other words, the New Testament makes no distinction between scripture and the words of God. Therefore, scripture *is* the Word of God and as such inerrant.

There are, however, severe problems with the concept of inerrancy. A major criticism is that the biblical passages cited in defence of inerrancy simply fail to perform the task demanded of them. Close scrutiny of perhaps the most important of the 'inerrancy texts', namely 2 Tim 3.16, must make us doubt whether this passage really sheds any light on the question of the inerrancy of the Bible. William Abraham has drawn attention to the relative insignificance of 2 Timothy and questioned the legitimacy of attempting to build a biblical conception of inspiration on such a relatively unimportant part of the New Testament.[89] A still more serious problem is that inspiration is clearly not the author's main area of concern. A careful reading of the passage in its broader context will reveal that the author's real purpose is not to offer a theory of inspiration but to make clear the significance of scripture for the moral and spiritual life of the Christian. In view of the fact that its reference to inspiration is little more than an incidental remark, 2 Tim 3.16 seems an insufficient foundation upon which to base a theology of biblical inerrancy.

The strongest argument against the attempt to base a doctrine of inerrancy on 2 Tim 3.16, however, is that nowhere in the passage is the claim made that every word of the Bible is the literal Word of God and must therefore be

[88] Warfield, *Inspiration and Authority of the Bible*, p. 299. See also Alan M. Stibbs, 'The witness of Scripture to its inspiration', in Henry (ed.), *Revelation and the Bible*, pp. 105–18, esp. 115–16.
[89] Abraham, *Divine Inspiration*, pp. 92–3.

utterly free of error. Such an understanding of the text can be arrived at only by presupposing that inspiration entails inerrancy. This connection, however, is not made by the author of 2 Timothy, who merely says, 'All scripture is inspired by God', and makes no mention of inerrancy. It seems clear, then, that 2 Tim 3.16 is not capable of bearing the weight that has been placed upon it by conservative scholars and that it provides insufficient support for a doctrine of the inerrancy of scripture. The argument only works if we assume that inerrancy is a characteristic of inspiration. This is not, however, a connection which 2 Tim 3.16 makes.

2 Pet 1.21 also seems to be incapable of providing a convincing basis for biblical inerrancy. Despite Warfield's ingenious interpretation of this passage, all that 2 Peter claims is that prophecy originates from God. This is *not* the same as asserting that the Bible claims inerrancy for itself. The passage makes no mention of the idea that every word of the Bible must be literally the Word of God and free from error. The point the author of 2 Peter wishes to make is merely that prophecy is not a human invention or achievement but comes about as the result of divine initiative.

The use of John 14.26 in defence of inerrancy is due to a confusion over the meaning and nature of the term 'error'. The term seems to be used in two different senses by supporters of inerrancy.[90] On the one hand, the term is employed to describe a belief or proposition originally believed to be true, but now known to be incorrect. Applied to the Bible, 'error' in this sense denotes an assertion fully in harmony with the biblical world-view, but which is no longer acceptable in the light of modern scientific develop-

[90] See Achtemeier, *Inspiration of Scripture*, pp. 61–2, for a discussion of this point.

ments. On the other hand, the term 'error' is understood to mean the deliberate and malicious misleading of one person by another – the 'teacher' consciously imparts to the learner something the former knows to be a falsehood. By conflating these two different understandings of error, we arrive at the position that an 'error' arising from a superseded world-view indicates a deliberate misleading of human beings on the part of a mischievous Holy Spirit. Since this is a conclusion no Christian could possibly accept, so the argument runs, we are committed to biblical inerrancy. However, such an argument is convincing, only if we are prepared to make an unwarrantable connection between 'error' and 'malicious deception'.

It is also highly questionable how appropriate the conservative conception of error is to the Bible. As Achtemeier points out, 'The fundamental concept of truth in the Bible is not conformity between statement and "objective reality", but rather reliability, dependability. The opposite of such truth is not error, but fickleness or deliberate deception.'[91] Consequently,

> the real test of truth in Scripture is whether the respondent, confronted with a new situation, used the available traditions responsibly to encourage belief in the reliability of God and the dependability of his promises, not whether in some simile the figure happened to accord with what we take to be the truth in the realm from which the simile was drawn.[92]

Problems also arise with the attempt to employ Jesus' citations of scripture in defence of inerrancy. There are a number of assumptions contained in the logic of this

[91] Ibid., p. 148.
[92] Ibid.

argument that need to be tested. For instance, does Jesus' divinity entail omniscience? Of still greater significance is the fact that the interpretation of the passages that allegedly support inerrancy is frequently strained and often does violence to the fundamental thrust of the text. Thus John 10.35 is not concerned with the question of the inspiration of the Bible but with the status of Jesus and the nature of his relationship with the Father. Jesus' employment of scripture is subordinate to this. Similarly, a defence or promulgation of a doctrine of inspiration is not the main concern of Matt 5.17–18. On the contrary, Jesus' discussion of the status of the Old Testament is clearly subordinate to his ethical teaching. Furthermore, the passage can surely not be employed to show that Jesus held the Old Testament to be inerrant. As Abraham rightly points out,

> To press this from the text of Matt 5:17–18 is to over-interpret. Jesus did not hold to a flat view of the Old Testament. He certainly held that it expressed the will of God, but this must be read sensitively. There is a genuine dialectical relation between Jesus and the Old Testament; there is both a 'yes' and a 'no' in his use of it, rather than an unqualified 'yes'.[93]

To put this another way, we could say that Jesus did not hold to the letter of the law but to its spirit. His affirmation of the law stems from his conviction that it expresses the will of God. His fulfilment of the law stems from his awareness that the will of God can be expressed more fully in other forms. Jesus' willingness to rephrase the law or even to ignore or abrogate it when he thought necessary (e.g., Matt 5.21–45; Mark 10.2–9; 7.14–19) indicates that he

[93] Abraham, *Divine Inspiration*, p. 102.

did not see himself bound to a literal reading of the scriptures.

These various biblical passages, then, are unable to do the job required of them; they provide insufficient support for the view that the Bible claims that it is divinely inspired and inerrant. Furthermore, there are several good reasons for rejecting the very principle of allowing Jesus' view of scripture to determine our understanding of the inspiration of the Bible. Although Jesus clearly recognizes the scriptures as authoritative, it is by no means clear what writings he had in mind. The problem is that we do not know what writings comprised the scriptures at this period. There is no doubt that the concept of a body of authoritative writings that were normative for Israel's religious life had come into existence by the time of Jesus, but the precise boundaries of this collection of writings are uncertain. In other words, all that can be proved on the basis of Jesus' references to the scriptures is that he regarded them as originating from God and as authoritative for our religious life. This in itself, however, does not amount to a theory of inspiration. As Abraham rightly points out, 'We need to distinguish sharply between seeing the Bible as normative and seeing the Bible as verbally inspired.'[94]

What of the New Testament's citation of passages from the Old Testament as if they had been spoken directly by God? Do such passages provide evidence for the claim that inerrancy is a fundamental presupposition in the biblical texts? Does the fact that the New Testament makes no distinction between scripture and the words of God mean that scripture *is* the Word of God and as such inerrant? The problem here is that although these passages make clear that the New Testament writers believed that the Old Testament originated from God, they provide no direct,

[94] Ibid., p. 97.

unequivocal support for the doctrine of inerrancy.

The most powerful argument against biblical inerrancy, however, is that it fails to do justice to the phenomena of the Bible. A close examination of the Bible will reveal the existence of a multitude of grammatical errors, awkwardness of style, inconsistencies and downright mistakes. Lev 11.6 and Deut 14.7, for example, both describe the hare as a ruminant. This is quite simply wrong and no exegetical ingenuity can make it right. Similarly, in Matt 27.9–10 Matthew quotes a passage which he claims is from Jeremiah, but which is in fact from Zech 11.12–13. Alongside such errors, there are also innumerable inconsistencies in the Bible. A classic example is the discrepancy in the accounts of who instigated David's census. In 2 Sam 24.1–2 we are told that it is God who incites David to take a census of Israel and Judah. In 1 Chron 21.1–2, however, it is Satan who incites David to carry out the census. It is difficult to imagine a more fundamental internal contradiction in the Bible than this! Another example of biblical inconsistency is that whereas in 2 Sam 10.18 we are told that 'David slew of the Syrians the men of seven hundred chariots', we learn in the Chronicler's description of the very same battle that seven *thousand* men were killed (1 Chron 19.18). Many other examples of this kind could be cited. Their significance is that they seem to undermine the conservative claim that the Bible is free from error.

Supporters of biblical inerrancy are not unaware of the biblical inconsistencies and errors outlined above and have attempted to develop strategies for dealing with them.

The harmonization of contradictory biblical passages

Much of conservative exegesis is devoted to finding ways of harmonizing apparently contradictory biblical passages. A good example of this is Lindsell's attempt to harmonize the four Gospel accounts of Peter's denial of Jesus.[95] According to Mark 14.30, 72, Peter denied Jesus three times before the cock had crowed for the second time. According to Matt 26.34, 74; Luke 22.34, 60 and John 13.38, 18.27, however, Peter denied Jesus before the *first* cockcrow. Lindsell reconciles these apparently contradictory accounts by claiming that Peter denied Jesus *six* times. Peter's first three denials preceded the single cockcrow mentioned by Matthew, Luke and John. The second three denials are those recorded by Mark, which took place before the cock crowed for the second time.[96]

There are, however, severe problems with the principle of harmonization. First, as Achtemeier points out, Lindsell has not proved the accuracy and therefore inerrancy of the four Gospel accounts but has 'convincingly demonstrated that none of the four is inerrant, since none of them know what *really* happened, i.e., six denials'.[97] A second problem with harmonization is that many of the harmonizations proposed by conservative Christians quite simply stretch the reader's credulity to breaking-point.[98]

The theory of original autographs

A further strategy for dealing with the apparent errors and inconsistencies in the Bible is the theory of original autographs.[99] According to this theory, it is not in the

[95] Lindsell, *Battle for the Bible*, pp. 174–6.

[96] For an alternative attempt to reconcile the two accounts, see Archer, 'Alleged errors and discrepancies in the original manuscripts of the Bible', in Geisler, *Inerrancy*, pp. 65–7.

[97] Achtemeier, *Inspiration of Scripture*, p. 67.

[98] See James Barr, *Fundamentalism* (London: SCM Press, 1977), pp. 55–72.

[99] Among the proponents of this view are Warfield, 'The inerrancy of the original autographs', in *Selected Shorter Writings of Benjamin B. Warfield*, ed. John E. Meeter (Nutley, NJ: Presbyterian and Reformed Publishing Company, 1973), vol. 2; Bahnsen, 'The

present copies that the inspiration of the biblical texts lies but in the original autographs, i.e., the original documents composed by the biblical writers. Any 'errors' present in the Bible are due to the failure of scribes to copy accurately these original texts. As Hodge and Warfield put it,

> the historical faith of the church has always been that all the affirmations of Scripture of all kinds . . . are without error, when the *ipsissima verba* of the original autographs are ascertained and interpreted in their natural and intended sense . . . No 'error' can be asserted, therefore, which cannot be proved to have been aboriginal in the text.[100]

Bahnsen makes clear the advantages of centring inerrancy in the original autographs:

> restricting inerrancy to the autographa *enables us to consistently confess the truthfulness of God* – and that is quite important indeed! Inability to do so would be quite theologically damaging. Only with an inerrant autograph can we avoid attributing error to the God of truth. An error in the original would be attributable to God Himself, because He, in the pages of Scripture, takes responsibility for the very words of the biblical authors. Errors in copies, however, are the sole

inerrancy of the autographa', in Geisler, *Inerrancy*, pp. 149–93; Young, *Thy Word is Truth*, pp. 56–7; Wenham, *Christ and the Bible*, p. 186; Nicole, 'The Nature of Inerrancy', in Nicole and Ramsey Michaels, *Inerrancy and Common Sense*, esp. pp. 73–8; Douglas Stuart, 'Inerrancy and textual criticism', in Nicole and Ramsey Michaels, *Inerrancy and Common Sense*, pp. 97–117; 101–2; Pinnock, *Biblical Revelation*, pp. 81–6; Henry, *God, Revelation and Authority*, vol. 4, § 9.

[100] Archibald A. Hodge and Benjamin B. Warfield, 'Inspiration', in *The Presbyterian Review* 7 (April 1881), 227, 236, 238; quoted in Bahnsen, 'The inerrancy of the autographa', in Geisler, *Inerrancy*, p. 156.

responsibility of the scribes involved, in which case God's veracity is not impugned.[101]

The restriction of inspiration to original autographs is problematic, however, since they are no longer in our possession. Furthermore, there is no evidence in the Bible to support the theory. Indeed, what evidence we have seems to argue strongly against it. The reference in 2 Tim 3.16 to the inspiration of scripture, for example, is – in view of the fact that the Old Testament quotations in 2 Timothy come from the Septuagint – most likely a reference not to original autographs but to the Septuagint version of the Old Testament. That is, far from restricting inspiration to the original autographs, the author of 2 Timothy attributes it to a Greek translation of the Hebrew scriptures.[102] Another problem with the theory is that if God went to the trouble of ensuring that the original autographs were free of error, why did he not also ensure that all subsequent copies of these autographs remained inerrant?

Further grounds for rejecting the theory of original autographs emerge when we inquire into the theological consequences of such a theory. If we take the autograph theory seriously, we are forced to ask what use is the present text of the Bible. Supporters of the autograph theory meet this objection by arguing that the present Bible reflects enough of the original autographs to allow it to function as the inspired Word of God. Pinnock comments that

[101] Bahnsen, 'The inerrancy of the autographa,' in Geisler, *Inerrancy*, p. 179; original emphasis.

[102] For an Evangelical response to this point, see Nicole, 'The nature of inerrancy', in Nicole and Ramsey Michaels, *Inerrancy and Common Sense*, pp. 78–80. Nicole argues that 'Any translation is entitled to acceptance as the Word of God to the extent that it corresponds to the original' (p. 79).

> Our Bibles are the Word of God to the extent that they reflect the Scripture as originally given; and because it is clear that they are virtually identical to it, it is also correct to regard them as virtually infallible themselves.[103]

The problem with this argument, however, is that if our present, 'errant' version of the Bible is capable of mediating God's saving Word, then the theory of autographs would seem to be redundant.

The illegitimacy of biblical criticism

As a result of the weakness and sheer implausibility of some defences of inerrancy, some of its supporters have adopted a more subtle and sophisticated approach and attack the presuppositions upon which historical criticism is based.[104] This attack can take one of two forms. First, defenders of inerrancy may attack biblical criticism as 'unscientific' on the grounds that it fails to study its object in a manner appropriate to the nature of that object. The Bible, it is argued, has a supernatural source. Consequently, by treating the Bible without reference to this source by bracketing out the possibility of the personal intervention of God and dealing with the Bible like any other work, the biblical critic is being untrue to the nature

[103] Pinnock, *Biblical Revelation*, p. 86; cf. Henry, *God, Revelation and Authority*, vol. 2, p. 14.

[104] For a representative of this position, see J. Barton Payne, 'Higher criticism and biblical inerrancy,' in Geisler, *Inerrancy*, pp. 83–113. Geisler attributes the decline of belief in inerrancy to Baconian inductivism, Hobbesian materialism, Spinozan rationalism, Humean sceptical empiricism, Kantian agnosticism and Kierkegaardian existentialism, all of which have combined to create a climate hostile to the doctrine of biblical inerrancy: Geisler, 'The philosophical presuppositions of biblical errancy,' in Geisler, *Inerrancy*, pp. 305–34.

of the object of his or her study. The presuppositions of those engaged in the sort of historical criticism which exposes alleged errors in the Bible, it is claimed, are not those of faith but those of unbelief. Their interpretation of the Bible and subsequent discovery of errors must thus be rejected, for their exegesis proceeds from illegitimate presuppositions. As Pinnock puts it, 'Criticism must be squarely rooted within the Christian faith, and be aware of the Biblical self-attestation. The assured results which are supposed to cripple infallibility are little more than the dubious assumption that Scripture may contain errors.'[105] In other words, because biblical critics have presupposed the existence of errors in the Bible, they naturally find them. Readers of the Bible who have faith as their fundamental presupposition will uncover no such errors.

This argument can be described as an application to the Bible of the principle that it is not reason but faith that must provide the starting-point for theology. There is much to be said for this approach with regard to the question of the human being's relation to God, for it could be argued that it is illegitimate to subject God to the strictures of human reason. Is it legitimate, however, to apply this principle to the Bible? The answer must surely be 'no', for the Bible is not a transcendent reality in itself, but expresses only the interaction of the transcendent reality that is God with humankind. Because one pole of this interaction is human, the Bible as a whole cannot have ascribed to it the status that belongs to God alone. The inerrantist approach is thus untrue to the nature of the God-human relationship.

The picture that emerges from our discussion is that the

[105] Pinnock, *A Defense of Biblical Infallibility* (Philadelphia: Presbyterian and Reformed, 1967), p. 30.

Bible's teaching concerning itself is very limited and certainly insufficient for a full doctrine of the inerrant inspiration of scripture. The New Testament passages we have discussed seem to be incapable of doing the work required of them by proponents of word-centred theories of inspiration. These passages certainly indicate that the biblical writers take scripture seriously and clearly regard it as coming from God in some way. Such passages also indicate, however, that the biblical authors were generally unconcerned with how this comes about. Indeed, the concept of inspiration is peripheral to the authors' other interests. There is certainly no hint whatsoever of any doctrine of inerrancy. This can only be extracted from these texts by presupposing its presence or by reading it into the texts, both of which are illegitimate exegesis. Furthermore, against the (dubious) evidence provided by such passages, New Testament texts can be cited that seem to argue *against* the doctrine of inerrant inspiration. In 1 Cor 7.10, 12, and 25, for example, Paul distinguishes between his own views and those of Christ. As Abraham points out, this means that 'we have . . . material in the New Testament which on its own clear and specific understanding cannot be construed as being given word for word by God. We must conclude therefore that the New Testament is not verbally inspired.'[106]

This does not mean, however, that the Bible has nothing to say about its own status and significance. On the contrary, there are numerous passages that make clear that the general view in the New Testament is that the Old Testament has come about as a result of the agency of the Divine Spirit.[107] All these passages are consonant with the

[106] Abraham, *Divine Inspiration*, p. 103.
[107] See, for example, Acts 1.16; 4.25; Heb 3.7.

picture that has already emerged from our discussion, namely that the Bible's own view of itself is that it comes from God and is authoritative for human beings. Other than this the Bible has little to say about its origins and certainly offers no full-blown doctrine of inspiration or theory of inerrancy.

In addition to these considerations, there are good reasons for doubting the theological usefulness of a doctrine of biblical inerrancy. The conservative concern with the inerrancy of the Bible is in danger of distracting us from the theological content of the Bible. The Bible's description of historical events, for example, is not carried out for the sake of providing an 'objective' account of these events, but to show how God is engaged in and guiding the history of the community of faith. Discrepancies over minor historical details such as troop numbers are simply irrelevant to the theological point that lies at the heart of the Bible's treatment of history. To put it another way, inerrancy in the sense in which conservatives employ the term is simply inappropriate for the sort of literature the Bible contains. As Achtemeier puts it, 'Such minute inerrancy may be appropriate, even necessary, for a telephone book or the instruction manual for a computer, but not for psalms of rejoicing, or letters to recalcitrant communities of faith, or apocalyptic visions, or parables.'[108] However, this does not mean that we must abandon the concept of biblical inerrancy, but rather that we should centre it not on historical or geographical details but on our relationship with God. As Burtchaell says, 'To be inerrant means not to wander, nor go astray, nor lose the path. It does not mean to sit down, but to forge forward with the assurance of not getting lost.'[109] Similarly, Goldingay comments,

[108] Achtemeier, *Inspiration of Scripture*, p. 148.
[109] Burtchaell, *Catholic Theories of Inspiration*, p. 299.

> In scripture . . . talk of the infallibility of the word of God implies a claim about its truth, not in the sense of factual correctness, since it is likely to be a statement that is not at present factually correct, but in the sense of its reliability and effectiveness. Scripture's own way of understanding the infallibility of God's word takes it as a statement of what will be, not of what is.[110]

We have seen in this chapter that there are several problems with the various word-centred theories of inspiration. The instrumental and dictation theories undermine human autonomy and seem unable to account for the diversity of the biblical literature. The verbal and plenary theories, apart from their own distinctive individual problems, fail because of their commitment to inerrancy, which, as we have seen, is not supported by the phenomena of the Bible. In the next chapter we shall consider whether the non-verbal approach is capable of constructing a more successful theology of inspiration than the word-centred approach.

[110] Goldingay, *Models of Scripture*, pp. 212–13.

3

Non-verbal theories of inspiration

The Enlightenment had a significant impact on theories of inspiration. For those influenced by the Enlightenment's emphasis on the primacy of autonomy and reason, the supernaturalism underlying word-centred theories of biblical inspiration was felt to be no longer tenable. This conviction was accompanied by an increasing consciousness of the historical nature and conditioning of the biblical texts and the awareness that the Bible contains contradictions, an outmoded world-view and material that appears to be unworthy of God. At the same time many of those who accepted the presence of problematic material in the Bible continued to feel that the Bible contained passages of such spiritual beauty and profundity that it seemed impossible that they should have originated from a merely human hand. Such theologians were thus confronted by the problem of reconciling the impact of scientific and historico-critical developments in our understanding of the Bible with a high doctrine of scripture. The way around this problem is to situate inspiration not in the letter of the text but in some other, non-verbal dimension of the biblical texts such as their conceptual content or the God-relationship which underlies and gives rise to the text of the Bible. We find a much greater diversity of views among adherents of non-verbal theories of inspiration than is the case with word-centred theories. This arises from disagreement concerning the nature of the non-verbal dimension in which biblical inspiration is held to reside. Despite their differences, however, non-verbal theories of inspiration have in common a rejection of word-based approaches to inspiration and a commitment to the view that biblical inspiration resides not in the words of the biblical text but in some allegedly deeper level or dimension believed to be contained within, beneath or behind the text. It is the slippage between this non-verbal dimension and its fixing in textual form by flawed human beings that accounts for the problematic material in the Bible. The following is a brief overview of such theories of inspiration.

Inspiration of the moral and spiritual teachings of the Bible

The inspiration of the Bible, it is argued, resides in its moral and spiritual teachings. Other material – historical, geographical, scientific – that appears alongside the moral and spiritual teachings has been drawn from the culture and world-view of the time and, although present in the Bible, is not strictly speaking part of the divine revelation. It is in this material that the inconsistencies and outmoded views of the Bible are to be found. Such flaws, however, do not affect the moral and spiritual teachings of the Bible, and it is in these teachings that the significance and inspired status of the Bible resides.

Such an argument is advanced by Charles Gore in his essay in *Lux Mundi*.[1] Gore argues for the presence of a general inspiration among the various peoples of the world. 'Every race has its special vocation', he writes, 'and we

[1] Charles Gore, 'The Holy Spirit and inspiration,' in Charles Gore (ed.), *Lux Mundi* (London: John Murray, 1890), pp. 313–62.

recognize in the great writers of each race the interpreters of that vocation.'[2] The inspiration of such individuals as Virgil, Aeschylus and Plato, however, is not attributable to purely human gifts, but is due to divine inspiration and, despite being obscured by human pride, wilfulness and pretentiousness, expresses a movement of the Divine Spirit. 'Thus every race', Gore concludes, 'has its inspiration and its prophets'.[3] The inspiration of the Jews, however, was of a different order, for 'the inspiration of the Jews was supernatural'.[4] But what does it mean to speak of supernatural inspiration and how does it differ from the general inspiration of the Greeks and Romans? The difference lies in the fact that whereas the inspired individuals of other nations were selected to be 'the school for humanity in any of the arts and sciences which involve the thought of God only indirectly', the Jews were selected in order to be the school of the 'fundamental restoration of man into that relation to God which sin had clouded or broken'. The consequence of this qualitatively different mission is that 'in the case of the Jews the inspiration is both in itself more direct and more intense, and also involves a direct consciousness on the part of its subjects'. This inspiration was, however, not spread uniformly among the members of the Jewish nation. Although this supernatural inspiration belonged to the Jewish people as a whole, it was particularly powerfully expressed in 'special men, prophets, psalmists, moralists, historians', who 'were thus the inspired interpreters of the Divine message to and in the race'.[5]

Gore attempts to pin down the nature of biblical

[2] Ibid., pp. 341–2.
[3] Ibid., pp. 342.
[4] Ibid.
[5] Ibid.

inspiration by comparing the Bible with other ancient literature. It is in the differences between the two bodies of literature that the inspiration of the Bible lies. Thus the inspired status of the creation narrative in Genesis lies in its teaching concerning the goodness of God, that the human being has a special relation to God, that human sin arises not from human nature but from disobedience, and that God has nevertheless not abandoned humankind but has given human beings a hope and a promise. 'These are the fundamental principles of true religion and progressive morality,' Gore tells us, 'and in these lies the supernatural inspiration of the Bible account of creation'.[6]

Gore conducts a similar interpretation of the remainder of the Old Testament. In the rest of Genesis 'the primary and certain meaning of its inspiration' is expressed in the fact that 'the first traditions of the race are all given there *from a special point of view*', namely from the viewpoint that 'everything is presented to us as illustrating God's dealings with man'.[7] The inspiration of the historical works lies not in their being motivated by the desire to promote the glory of Jewish nation or by interest in mere historical fact; it resides in their concern 'to keep before the chosen people the record of how God has dealt with them'.[8] It is the spiritual significance that the Old Testament historians see in the history of Israel which gives their works their inspired character: 'The inspiration of the recorder lies . . . primarily in this, that he sees the hand of God in the history and interprets His purpose'.[9] The inspiration of the psalmists, on the other hand, is situated in the fact that their 'poetic faculty is directed to one great end, to reveal

[6] Ibid., p. 344.
[7] Ibid.; original emphasis.
[8] Ibid., p. 344.
[9] Ibid., p. 351.

the soul in its relation to God, in its exultations and in its self-abasements'.

However, it is prophetic inspiration which provides us, Gore maintains, with 'the most obvious and typical instances of inspiration'.[10] 'The prophets', he writes, 'make a direct claim to be the instruments of the Divine Spirit.'[11] This divine use of the prophets does not override their human faculties but 'intensifies them'. As a result of divine inspiration, the prophets 'see deeper under the surface of life what God is doing, and therefore further into the future what He will do'. This 'predictive knowledge' is general in character. It does not extend to definite predictions of future events but speaks of that 'to which things tend'.[12]

Finally, Gore points to the organic wholeness of the Old Testament as an indication of the Old Testament's divine origins:

> Thus there is built up for us in the literature of a nation, marked by an unparalleled unity of purpose and character, a spiritual fabric, which in its result we cannot but recognize as the action of the Divine Spirit. A knowledge of God and of the spiritual life gradually appears, not as the product of human ingenuity, but as the result of Divine communication: and the outcome of this communication is to produce an organic whole which postulates a climax not yet reached, a redemption not yet given, a hope not yet satisfied.[13]

On these grounds Gore concludes that 'In this general

[10] Ibid., p. 345.
[11] Ibid., pp. 345–6.
[12] Ibid., p. 346.
[13] Ibid.

sense at least no Christian ought to feel a difficulty in believing, and believing with joy, in the inspiration of the Old Testament.'[14] In addition to this, there is a further guarantee of the inspiration of the Bible, namely Christ: 'Christ, the goal of Old Testament development, stands forth as the test and measure of its inspiration.'[15]

In the New Testament, Gore points out, 'There is not, except perhaps in the case of the Apocalypse, any sign of an inspiration to write, other than the inspiration which gave power to teach.'[16] This raises the question of what constitutes apostolic inspiration. For Gore the inspiration of the Apostles lies in their having been trained by Christ to communicate his divine message. Christ was concerned that 'His revelation should be, without material alloy, communicated to the Church which was to enshrine and perpetuate it.'[17] Consequently, 'He spent His chief pains on the training of His apostolic witnesses' in order to 'prepare them to receive the Holy Ghost Who, after He was gone, was to be poured out upon them to qualify them to bear His witness among men.'[18] The inspiration of the apostles, then, is 'an endowment which enables men of all ages to take their teaching as representing, and not misrepresenting, His teaching and Himself.'[19] That is, their inspiration lies in their authority and ability to communicate and interpret Christ to the world.

But what of the New Testament writings that were not composed by Apostles, such as, for example, the Gospel of Luke? Such writers had not received Christ's training in the communication and preservation of his teaching, so

[14] Ibid., pp. 346–7.
[15] Ibid., p. 347.
[16] Ibid.
[17] Ibid.
[18] Ibid.
[19] Ibid.

where does their inspiration lie, if they are indeed inspired? Gore argues that the inspiration of such writers

> was part of the whole spiritual endowment of their life which made them the trusted friends of the Apostles, and qualified them to be the chosen instruments to record their teaching, in the midst of a Church whose quick and eager memory of 'the tradition' would have acted as a check to prevent any material error creeping into the record.[20]

Gore also addresses the question of what we have described as 'subjective inspiration', namely the factors that enable or allow the reader of the scriptures to accept them as divinely inspired. On the basis of 2 Tim 3.16 Gore claims that 'To believe in the inspiration of Holy Scripture is to put ourselves to school with every part of the Old Testament, as of the New.' Indeed, 'we should set ourselves to study what we like less, till that too has had its proper effect in moulding our conscience and character'.[21] The more we 'put ourselves to school' under scripture and allow ourselves to be formed by the teaching it contains, Gore argues, 'the more confidently it is treated as the inspired guide of faith and conduct', and 'the more the experience and appreciation of its inspiration grows upon us, so that to deny or doubt it comes to mean to deny or to doubt a matter plain to the senses'.[22]

Gore deals with the problematic material of the Bible in a number of ways. He points to the human limitations of the biblical writers. Although the prophets had insight into God's workings in history and his purposes for the future,

[20] Ibid., pp. 348–9.
[21] Ibid., p. 349.
[22] Ibid., p. 351.

this was only an insight into the general course of God's activity in history and did not provide them with information as to the specific times at which divine action could be expected. It is because the prophets have insight only into the general course of God's activity in history that they may be mistaken with regard to the specific times at which divine action is to take place. As Gore puts it, 'The prophetic inspiration is thus consistent with erroneous anticipations as to the circumstances and the opportunity of God's self-revelation, just as the apostolic inspiration admitted of S. Paul expecting the second coming of Christ within his own life-time.'[23]

Gore also argues for gradations of inspiration in scripture. The biblical writers experienced different intensities of inspiration. At one extreme there is the prophet, whose inspiration is 'direct, continuous, absorbing'.[24] At the other extreme there is the author of Ecclesiastes, whose inspiration

> is such as to lead him to ponder on all the phases of a worldly experience, passing through many a false conclusion, and cynical denial, till at the last his thought is led to unite itself to the great stream of Divine movement by finding the only possible solution of the problems of life in the recognition of God, and in obedience to Him.[25]

A further reason for the presence of problematic material in the Bible is that the Spirit does not override the humanity of the biblical writers but works through it. As Gore puts it, 'the supernatural fertilizes and does not

[23] Ibid., p. 346.
[24] Ibid., p. 342.
[25] Ibid., p. 343.

annihilate the natural'. Indeed, the Spirit works through and in the human medium in a way that parallels the relationship between the divinity and humanity of Christ. In neither case is the humanity destroyed, but is given its dues. Just as Jesus' humanity did not impair his divinity, so too the presence of human elements in the Bible does not detract from its divine inspiration. In Gore's words, 'As the humanity of Christ is none the less a true humanity for being conditioned by absolute oneness with God, so the human activity is none the less free, conscious, rational, because the Spirit inspires it.'[26]

It is this union of the divine with the human in scripture that accounts for the diversity of biblical literature and the presence of problematic material in the Bible. God made use of the different human qualities and gifts of the biblical writers in the composition of the Bible and it is these diverse human qualities and gifts that account for the different types of literature in the Bible.[27] The problematic material in the Bible is due to the fact that, although 'inspiration certainly means the illumination of the judgement of the recorder', this does not mean that the biblical writers were immune to the historical and cultural context in which they lived.[28]

The advantage of Gore's approach is that it allows us to retain a divine input into a biblical text without having to attribute errors, inconsistencies or outmoded world-views to God. Such flaws are simply due to the biblical writers' choice of words, which was of course moulded by their cultural and historical situation and the language which they had at their disposal. Gore also has the important insight that the inspiration of scripture becomes apparent

[26] Ibid.
[27] Ibid., pp. 355–6.
[28] Ibid., p. 354.

only in so far as we engage with the Bible and apply it to ourselves. We are to put ourselves to school under scripture and employ it for our spiritual education. As we do so, the inspired status of scripture will become ever more evident.

Gore's understanding of inspiration faces the same problem as all non-verbal theories, namely, that of establishing clear criteria to distinguish what belongs to the central moral and spiritual teachings of the Bible and what is merely material due to the culture in which these teachings were given. Gore seems to have no difficulty in distinguishing between the two bodies of material, but is vague about the criteria for making such a distinction. Without such criteria, however, we shall be unable to establish whether the doctrine of incarnation, for example, is a divinely inspired teaching or merely a view of Jesus due to the now outmoded world-view of the early Church.

Inspiration as selection

In his book, *The Divine Inspiration of Holy Scripture*, Sanday sees inspiration as part of God's broader purpose for humankind and subsumes it under the doctrine of Providence: 'The true method by which Divine Providence has worked is indicated in that most pregnant phrase of St. Paul's, "The purpose of God according to selection".'[29] This involves the selection of Israel as the instrument for the carrying out of the divine purpose. Within this selected people there are individuals who are specially chosen by God to communicate his will.

> Just as one particular branch of one particular stock was chosen to be in a general sense the recipient of a

[29] William Sanday, *Inspiration* (London: Longmans, Green & Co., 1896), p. 422.

> clearer revelation than was vouchsafed to others, so within that branch certain individuals were chosen to have their hearts and minds moved in a manner more penetrating and more effective than their fellows, with the result that their written words convey to us truths about the nature of God and His dealings with man which other writings do not convey with equal fulness, power, and purity. We say that this special moving is due to the action upon those hearts and minds of the Holy Spirit. And we call that action Inspiration.[30]

Inspiration, then, is the state of being selected by God to carry out his purpose.

Of course, such a definition of inspiration needs further development, for it says nothing about the manner in which inspiration functions, nor does it explain how we are to recognize genuine instances of inspiration. To answer these questions, a deeper analysis of inspiration is required. Sanday takes the prophets as the starting-point for this analysis, 'because in the Prophets not only the fact of Inspiration but the manner of it are most evident'.

The prophets were clearly convinced that

> they were instruments or organs of the Most High, and that the thoughts which arose in their minds about Him and His Will, and the commands and exhortations which they issued in His Name, really came at His prompting, and were really invested with His authority.[31]

But why should we accept the prophets' view of

[30] Ibid., p. 127.
[31] Ibid., p. 394.

themselves and their calling? According to Sanday, the only alternative to accepting the prophets' claim to be divinely inspired is to regard their inspiration 'as a product of mental disease or delusion'. Sanday rejects this explanation on the grounds that it is impossible to envisage mental disease or delusion stretching from generation to generation through the whole line of prophets. Furthermore, the charge of mental disease

> is refuted in advance by the contents of the prophecies themselves, which, if once we allow that there is a God, make those affirmations about Him which the world has pronounced to be the best and truest, and which it has taken as the centre of its beliefs to this day. A world-wide religion which for more than thirty centuries has been taking increasing hold on the most highly developed races could not have its origin in mere mental disease.[32]

Since the claims of the prophets cannot be attributed to mental illness or delusion, we are left, in Sanday's judgement, with no other alternative than to accept the validity and veracity of their claim to be inspired. Having established the genuineness of the prophetic claim, Sanday then offers the following definition of inspiration: it is 'the gift by which God Himself spake through them and made them the channels of the communication of His Will to men'.[33]

This understanding of inspiration derived from the prophets can also be applied to the Law. This is because, having established the nature of inspiration, 'we can argue backwards to one like Moses, of whom the documents are

[32] Ibid.
[33] Ibid., pp. 395–6.

too late to give us a perfectly adequate portraiture'.[34] That is, since Moses was the founder of the religion which gave rise to the classical prophets, we can attribute to him the same kind of inspiration found in the case of the prophets. Furthermore, since it was Moses' teaching which gave rise to the Pentateuch, we can attribute divine inspiration to the law. The conclusion Sanday draws from his analysis is that the law and the prophets constitute 'primary inspiration' and it is from them that we gain knowledge of God and his will.

Once the nature of prophetic inspiration has been established, it can be used as a means for assessing the inspired status of the other books of the Old Testament. The historical works, the psalms and the wisdom literature are inspired by virtue of their dependence upon the primary revelation contained in the law and the prophets. Their inspiration, however, is what Sanday terms 'secondary inspiration', because they do not themselves provide any new insights but are concerned merely to apply the teaching of the law and the prophets to every aspect of human life. That is, these texts are inspired because they are an extension of the inspired message of the law and the prophets to other areas of life. They are, as Sanday puts it, 'the practical commentary upon revelation, pressing it home into the chinks and crannies of daily life'.[35] However, because they are dependent on the primary revelation given in the law and the prophets, the inspiration found in the historical works, the psalms and wisdom literature of the Old Testament is only secondary in nature.

On the basis of this analysis Sanday puts forward two explanations of the errors and inconsistencies contained in the Bible. First, Sanday makes use of his distinction

[34] Ibid., p. 396.
[35] Ibid., p. 397.

between primary and secondary inspiration to account for those elements of the Bible that seem to lack inspiration. Such elements are due to their distance from primary inspiration. That is, the level of inspiration of the biblical material diminishes according to how far removed it is from primary inspiration in much the same way as light and heat grow weaker as they travel further from the sun. From this Sanday concludes that 'there are some books in which the Divine element is at the *maximum* and others in which it is at the *minimum*'.[36] Those works in which inspiration is at a minimum are more prone to contain errors and inconsistencies, for in such works the human input is greater.

Sanday's second explanation of the errors of the Bible is based on his understanding of inspiration as selection. 'This very idea of selection', he tells us, 'implies also infinite gradation and variety of tone and shade.'[37] It is this gradation that accounts for the errors of the Bible, for each expression of biblical truth bears vestiges of the lower stage from which it has emerged.

> Every higher phenomenon has its roots in something lower; the superior grows out of the inferior. But they must needs bear some traces of their origin: the plant which is rooted in the earth will of necessity have some earth cling to its roots. So the very grandest and sublimest of Divine revelations have been made through human *media*; and from time to time we are reminded that the *media* are human.[38]

[36] Ibid., p. 398.
[37] Ibid., p. 422.
[38] Ibid., pp. 422–3.

When all the various and different levels of divine inspiration in the Bible are taken together, however, it becomes clear, Sanday claims, that they all form a coherent whole and constitute *in toto* a clear expression of the Divine purpose. He writes:

> But if we take a wider range, and look at the diversified products of this individual inspiration, and see how they combine together, so as to be no longer detached units but articulated members in a connected and coherent scheme, we must needs feel that there is something more than the individual minds at work; they are subsumed, as it were, in the operation of a larger Mind, that central Intelligence which directs and gives unity and purpose to the scattered movements and driftings of men.[39]

It is this combining of the individual expressions of inspiration into a greater whole that, Sanday claims, constitutes the link between traditional and inductive theories, for both theories bring out the Divine Mind expressed in the biblical writings. The difference between the two is that 'the follower of the older view of inspiration did this with more emphasis and less caution', for he ignored the distinctive perspectives of the individual biblical writers. However, Sanday adds,

> if he clearly recognizes the distinction between what can be verified and what cannot be verified, he is not called upon either to abandon all that a pious fancy has accumulated in the past or to desist from the employment of like methods in the future.[40]

[39] Ibid., p. 402.
[40] Ibid., p. 406.

The strength of Sanday's position is that by positing a gradation of inspiration in the biblical writings, he is able to reconcile the concept of inspiration with the results of modern biblical scholarship. The weaknesses of his theory of inspiration are that it does not make clear how primary inspiration comes about and how claims to inspiration are to be justified. He claims, as we saw earlier, that the inspiration is 'a real objective action of the Divine upon the human', but does not explain how this divine action takes place.

The inspiration of the biblical images

In his 1948 Bampton lectures, published as *The Glass of Vision*, Austin Farrer proposes that inspiration should be situated in the *images* of the Bible. The biblical images, particularly those associated with Christ, mediate 'supernatural knowledge', by which he means knowledge

> which transposed us, as it were, to the divine centre of such activity: which gave us to know, not the bare idea of such a centre, but anything about the way in which the life there lived is exercised and enjoyed at its own divine level: anything which reveals to us the activity of God in God.[41]

Supernatural knowledge, then, is knowledge of things as they appear from the divine centre that is God. It is a participation in the divine view of things.

This supernatural knowledge is the result of the supernatural action of God on the human mind, which, Farrer writes, 'bestows an apprehension of divine mysteries,

[41] Farrer, *Glass of Vision*, p. 30.

inaccessible to natural reason, reflection, intuition or wit'.[42] Such supernatural knowledge is to be found in the scriptures, above all in the New Testament. 'In the New Testament', Farrer writes, 'we can as it were overhear men doing supernatural thinking of a privileged order, with pens in their hands'.[43] This supernatural thinking manifests itself in images.

These supernatural, revelatory images are due to divine initiative. God gives us the images, above all in the Person of Christ, in whom 'the revelation of deity to manhood is absolutely fulfilled'.[44] But these images do not come upon us wholly unawares, as it were. Preparation for the revealed images is provided by means of the archetypes of the Old Testament, archetypes that arise from fundamental experiences of human existence such as birth, growth, love, kingship, fatherhood and so on. Such archetypes, 'however heathenish they look, hold the promise of revelation',[45] for the Old Testament archetypes are forerunners of the revealed images and are transformed into images of the divine through Christ and the Holy Spirit.

The centre around which the biblical images revolve is, of course, Christ, and it is Christ himself, Farrer claims, who laid the foundations for the revelation-mediating images of the New Testament through the imagery he himself employed in his teaching. 'The thought of Christ Himself', Farrer writes, 'was expressed in certain dominant images', such as 'the Kingdom of God, which is the image of God's enthroned majesty'; the 'Son of man', which proposes 'the image of the dominion of a true Adam, begotten in the similitude of God, and made God's regent over all the works

[42] Ibid., p. 35.
[43] Ibid.
[44] Ibid., p. 39.
[45] Ibid., p. 105.

of his hands'; 'the image of Israel' and Christ's application to himself of 'the prophecies of a redemptive suffering for mankind attributed to Israel by Isaiah and Jewish tradition'; finally, Christ 'displayed, in the action of the supper, the infinitely complex and fertile image of sacrifice and communion, of expiation and covenant'.[46]

It is the task and responsibility of the apostolic writers under the guidance of the Spirit to unfold more fully the images revealed by and in Christ.[47] It is this that constitutes their inspiration:

> In the apostolic mind . . . the God-given images lived, not statically, but with an inexpressible creative force. The several distinct images grew together into fresh unities, opened out in new detail, attracted to themselves and assimilated further image-material: all this within the life of a generation. This is the way inspiration worked. The stuff of inspiration is living images.[48]

We can appreciate the inspiration of the Bible only in so far as we are moved by the biblical images. If we adopt the medieval scholastic approach and comb the Bible for theological propositions or follow 'the modern tendency . . . to seek after historical record', 'we close our ears to the voice of Scripture' and 'fail . . . to find either the voice of God, or the substance of supernatural mystery'.[49] Nor should we reduce the images to their conceptual content: 'Each image will have its own conceptual conventions, proper to the figure it embodies', which 'a single over-all

[46] Ibid., p. 42.
[47] Ibid., p. 41.
[48] Ibid., pp. 43–4.
[49] Ibid., p. 44.

conceptual analysis' will undermine.[50] The only appropriate way of relating to the images, then, is to immerse ourselves in them and allow them to move us.[51] As Farrer puts it, 'We have to listen to the Spirit speaking divine things: and the way to appreciate his speech is to quicken our own minds with the life of the inspired images.'[52]

As an example of how a biblical image can move the reader Farrer cites Gal 4.6: 'God sent forth the Spirit of his Son into our hearts, crying Abba, Father.' 'The Christian who reads this,' Farrer writes,

> considers the perfection of unique divine sonship, and stirs his heart to gratitude for the amazing gift of a share in it: he awes his mind with the thought that he is possessed by the Spirit of God, and is, in reality and in God's eyes, Christ towards his God and towards his neighbour: he deplores the darkness which commonly veils what now he sees in the clarity of faith, and the sin which falsifies it in act. He throws himself on the love of the Trinity, more patient with him than he is with himself, and silently operative to produce in him even such penitence and vision as now he has. All these motions of the soul take place within the field of the image: they do not pass out of it into the thin upper air of definition and speculation, nor down onto the flat ground of mere penitence and self-management.[53]

There are, however, many passages in the New Testament that cannot be categorized as images or as an

[50] Ibid., p. 45.
[51] Ibid., p. 51.
[52] Ibid., p. 44, cf., 51.
[53] Ibid., pp. 51–2.

apostolic unfolding of images. The New Testament contains material, such as Paul's discussion of now redundant problems in his letters, that have only historical interest for the modern reader. Consequently, 'to say that the apostolic mind was divinely inspired by the germination there of the image-seeds which Christ had sown, is not to give a plain and uniform account of the inspiration of the text of Scripture, comparable with the old doctrine of inerrant supernatural dictation'.[54] The conception of the Bible as a collection of images is thus unable to provide a comprehensive theory of inspiration that can be applied to the Bible as a whole. It is, however, no blemish, Farrer claims, if his image theory cannot provide a uniform conception of inspiration.

> What is vital is that we should have such a doctrine of Scripture as causes us to look for the right things in reading Scripture: above all, that we should look for the life-giving inspired word, and make the proper use of it when we have found it.[55]

Having established that 'divine truth is supernaturally communicated to men in an act of inspired thinking which falls into the shape of certain images',[56] the next issue that needs to be addressed is 'how it is that the images are able to signify divine realities'.[57] How do we know that the biblical images refer to a genuine reality and are not merely figments of the biblical writers' imagination? In our attempt to answer this question, Farrer points out, we are confronted by a special difficulty that is absent in our

[54] Ibid., p. 52.
[55] Ibid.
[56] Ibid., p. 57.
[57] Ibid.

knowledge of mundane things, namely the lack of an empirically accessible object by means of which we can check and verify the referential function of the image.[58] The problem is, as Farrer phrases it, that:

> We cannot by-pass the images to seize an imageless truth. Does this mean that our minds are simply given over to the images, bound hand and foot? Can we in any way criticize the images? Have we, outside them, any rule by which to regulate our intuition of what they mean?[59]

Farrer addresses this problem in several related ways. The coming alive of the images in our souls, he argues, is itself an indication of the reality to which they point. Indeed, such a stirring of the God-consciousness is essential, for

> apart from the presence in the soul of a foretaste or earnest of supernatural life, revealed truth is dumb to us. We may hear and read the verbal declaration of divine truth for years, and not apprehend the thing signified; when a motion of supernatural life stirs within us, then we have thing as well as word, and begin to apprehend.[60]

The movement in the soul under the pressure of the divine images, then, indicates an underlying reality responsible for prompting this movement.[61]

Still more is needed, however, in order to secure the

[58] Ibid., pp. 58, 73.
[59] Ibid., p. 110.
[60] Ibid., p. 59.
[61] Ibid., p. 60.

objective reality of that to which the images refer, for how do we know that that to which the supernatural movement of the soul points is God? The problem is that God is unique and consequently there is nothing with which he can be compared. We are thus prohibited from using the procedures we employ in dealing with mundane realities, namely that of comparing the images with the realities to which they refer and thereby checking the validity of the images and establishing that they do indeed refer to genuine realities.[62]

To solve this problem, Farrer turns to natural theology for assistance. Natural theology, he argues, provides us with a conception of God which can act as a means of identifying and recognizing the God who meets us in the revealed images. As Farrer puts it, 'Natural theology . . . provides a canon of interpretation which stands outside the particular matter of revealed truth.'[63] How natural theology achieves this is described by Farrer as follows:

> The subject of the revealed figurative sentences is God: they must, then, be so understood that God can be the subject of them: and natural theology supplies us with a notion of God, itself analogical, it is true, but . . . composed of natural, and criticized, analogies, so that it can be settled and defined by a rational process. When we use this idea of the supreme being as a canon to interpret revelation, we are not importing into revelation something which was originally absent from it. On the contrary: guided and assisted by revealed insight, the apostles plainly did exercise that apprehension of the infinite creator through the works of nature which is the substance of

[62] Ibid., p. 62.
[63] Ibid., p. 111.

natural knowledge.[64]

This raises the question of what revealed images contribute to our comprehension of God that was not present in the rational analogies of natural theology. Farrer seems to think that their contribution lies in a concretization of our conception and knowledge of God that came about through the apostles' witnessing to God's action in Christ:

> What God bestowed on them through Christ was revelation of God's particular action. They had not known before that God would send his Son for us men and our salvation, but they had known that God was God; and what they now learnt was not that some superhuman Father had sent his Son, but that God had done so.[65]

Farrer's theory of inspiration has a great deal going for it. By situating inspiration not in the text but in the images of the Bible, he is able to avoid the problems encountered by text-centred theories of inspiration. What is significant about the Bible is not so much the words but the images it contains and their power to initiate a supernatural movement in our souls. This leads to a second advantage of Farrer's theory, namely, his emphasis on the importance of the stirring of the God-consciousness. Only when the biblical images evoke a supernatural movement within us can we apprehend and appreciate the inspired nature of the Bible.

The problems with Farrer's position stem from the way he attempts to underpin his theory of images. To resort to natural theology to secure the objective reality of that to

[64] Ibid., p. 110.
[65] Ibid., pp. 110–11.

which the images refer is, in view of the ambiguity of the natural world and the controversial and problematic status of natural theology, an argument that will fail to convince many. The way forward, I will suggest in the next chapter, is to supplement Farrer's theory of images with Jaspers' concept of ciphers and situate the justification of inspiration not in natural theology but in the impact of the biblical images on human subjectivity.

The teacher model of inspiration

What we have termed the 'teacher model of inspiration' is advanced by William Abraham in his book *The Divine Inspiration of Holy Scripture*. Although he himself is from an Evangelical background, he believes that the adherents of the Evangelical understanding of inspiration have made 'two fatal mistakes. First of all they ignored the need to begin with human agents; instead they began, continued, and ended with God. Secondly, they failed to focus on inspiration; they focused instead on speaking.'[66] If we are to arrive at a contemporary, coherent and credible theory of inspiration, Abraham tells us, we must separate divine inspiration from divine speaking. This means that we should not take as our starting-point God's speech to the Old Testament prophets, which has been the traditional starting-point for discussion of inspiration, but must first clarify the meaning of inspiration with regard to human beings. That is, only when we have established what it means for one human being to inspire another can we decide in what way the term inspiration is applicable to God.[67]

[66] Abraham, *Divine Inspiration of Holy Scripture*, p. 62.
[67] Ibid., p. 61.

The analogy of human inspiration

Abraham sets the scene for the development of his own concept of inspiration by considering the 'inspiring' teacher. He notes that

> since the students will vary in ability, temperament, and interests, and since the intensity of their relationship may also vary, it is perfectly in order to speak of degrees of inspiration. There is no guarantee that inspiration will be uniform, flat, or even in its effects.[68]

Another feature worthy of note is that the teacher's inspiration of his or her pupils does not undermine their autonomy. There is no question of their being passive recipients of the teacher's inspired teaching. On the contrary, 'their native intelligence and talent will be greatly enhanced and enriched but in no way obliterated or passed over'.[69] Such inspiration is not, however, free from error: 'as there will be other influences and sources of inspiration at work upon them, there need be no surprise if, from the point of view of the teacher, they make mistakes'.[70] From this, Abraham concludes that the teacher's inspiration of his pupils is a 'polymorphous concept'. That is, inspiration is not one act alongside all the other acts that a teacher performs, such as supervision, teaching, publishing and so on, but is expressed in and through these acts.

But how do we recognize and measure whether and to what degree the teacher's pupils have been inspired? Although there are no hard and fast rules for detecting

[68] Ibid., p. 63.
[69] Ibid., p. 64.
[70] Ibid.

the effects of inspiration in the work produced by the pupils, the cumulative weight of several strands of evidence is normally enough to persuade us of the genuine existence of such effects. Such strands of evidence cited by Abraham are the 'testimony of the students', 'continuity of interests, outlook, and perhaps even style of approach to the issue in hand'.[71] This analysis of the example of the teacher allows Abraham to summarize what he regards as the key features of the concept of inspiration.

> First, inspiration is a unique, irreducible activity that takes place between personal agents, one of whom, the inspirer, makes a definite objective difference to the work of the other, the inspired, without obliterating or rendering redundant the native activity of the other. Secondly, inspiration is a polymorphous concept in that it is achieved in, with, and through other acts that an agent performs.[72]

These two features, Abraham claims, are minimal requirements in any analysis of inspiration and must therefore be preserved in any discussion of divine inspiration.[73]

Divine inspiration

Many of the insights gained in the analysis of the inspiring teacher can be applied to divine inspiration. Thus the insight that inspiration is a polymorphous concept is applicable to God. Like the teacher's inspiration of his pupils through his teaching, supervision, publications and so on, divine inspiration is not a single act alongside the

[71] Ibid.
[72] Ibid., p. 65.
[73] Ibid.

other divine acts but is present within and expressed through God's various dealings with humankind. Abraham writes:

> As a matter of logic, inspiration is a unique activity of God that cannot be defined in terms of his other acts or activity, but as a matter of fact he inspires in, with, and through his special revelatory acts and through his personal guidance of those who wrote and put together the various parts of the Bible.[74]

With regard to the Bible this means that 'It is through his revelatory and saving acts as well as through his personal dealings with individuals and groups that God inspired his people to write and collate what we now know as the Bible.'[75] Consequently, 'inspiration is not an activity that should be experientially separated from these other acts that God has performed in the past'.[76] What Abraham seems to be arguing, then, is that it is the impact of God's actions in human lives that constitutes inspiration. The people of ancient Israel were inspired by God's act of leading his people out of Egypt. Christians are inspired through God's act of becoming incarnate in Jesus of Nazareth and in raising Jesus from the dead. It is because they are 'moved' or 'inspired' by such acts that certain individuals record their experience of these acts, and it is this that leads to the Bible.

There are, however, significant ways in which the teacher analogy should be qualified when applying the term 'inspiration' to God. The first qualification is that whereas the teacher may not be aware of the inspirational

[74] Ibid., p. 67.
[75] Ibid.
[76] Ibid.

effect he or she is having on the pupils, 'because God is omniscient he will be aware that he is inspiring in a way that human agents are not, therefore inspiration on his part will be fully intentional'.[77] The second way in which the teacher model must be qualified is that 'because God is not an agent who can be located in the world of space and time, claims about the operation of his inspiration will be difficult to justify', for, as Abraham points out, 'We cannot, for example, show that God is active in the life of individuals or groups and thus is inspiring them with the same degree of ease as we do with human examples.'[78]

The other features of the teacher analogy can, Abraham believes, be retained, although he concedes that 'some may need to be restated in a different way'.[79] He then goes on to summarize his main points as follows:

> When we speak of the divine inspiration of the Bible it is legitimate to talk in terms of degrees of inspiration; to insist on the full, indeed heightened, use of native ability in the creation of style, content, vocabulary etc.; to note that there is no guarantee of inerrancy, since agents, even when inspired by God, can make mistakes; and finally to infer that inspiration will result, first, in some kind of unity within the biblical literature and secondly in the committal to writing of a reliable and trustworthy account of God's revelatory and saving acts for mankind.[80]

Abraham then goes on to argue that we can trust the Bible as a reliable account of God's saving acts, on the grounds of

[77] Ibid.
[78] Ibid.
[79] Ibid., p. 68.
[80] Ibid.

'God's unique status as the agent of inspiration in question'.[81] Since God is omniscient and infallible 'what he inspires will bear significant marks of truth and reliability'.[82]

On the basis of his analysis of inspiration, Abraham claims that it has become clear 'how far removed divine inspiration is from divine speaking'.[83] While admitting that these two phenomena are related by virtue of the fact that 'it is partly through speaking to various significant individuals that God inspires them and others to write, edit, collate and preserve the various traditions that go to make up the Bible', divine inspiration and divine speaking should not be regarded as identical. 'The relation between speaking and inspiration', Abraham goes on to argue, 'is contingent; there is no necessity for divine inspiration to be accomplished through divine speaking.'[84]

Abraham claims that his theory is able to do justice to several factors that undermined the traditional Evangelical view of inspiration. It 'is compatible with what is generally known about the origin and character of the biblical writings, . . . is genuinely at home with differences in style and viewpoint, with differences of emphasis and vocabulary and with the existence of borderline books in the canon', and 'also allows a substantial role for critical investigation'.[85] His theory is also able, Abraham claims, to deal with the alleged errors in the Bible. The reluctance on the part of Evangelical Christians to acknowledge such errors stems from their confusion of inspiration with divine speaking. If we can move away from the identification of inspiration with divine speaking, then this problem simply

[81] Ibid.
[82] Ibid.
[83] Ibid., p. 69.
[84] Ibid.
[85] Ibid.

falls away.

A further advantage of his understanding of inspiration, Abraham claims, is that it 'allows us to make use of this term outside the confines of the writing and production of the Bible'.[86] This avoids the idea, with which many Christians have long been unhappy, that inspiration has dried up since the closing of the canon. Abraham's understanding of inspiration 'can accommodate this insight without strain or artificiality', for by separating divine inspiration from divine speaking we can apply the term to individuals who live outside the period of the biblical revelation:

> We can talk of the ordinary Christian who is coping heroically with the burdens of life as being inspired by God. We can say the same for the faithful preacher and pastor persistently building up the people of God in the faith, for the extraordinary saint giving up all in self-sacrifice for the poor and the needy, and for the persuasive evangelist proclaiming the good news of the Gospel to the outside.[87]

To sum up Abraham's position, we could say that he wishes to reserve the term inspiration to describe those who are motivated to live their lives in the light of God's revelatory and saving acts in history. Some of these inspired individuals were responsible for writing the Bible, but essentially their position is no different from those who come later, who are also inspired by God's revelatory acts in history.

There are a number of criticisms that can be made of Abraham's theory of inspiration. Abraham himself notes

[86] Ibid., p. 71.
[87] Ibid.

that it might be objected that he has so stretched and diluted the concept of inspiration as to deprive it of significant use. He responds that such an objection is merely 'a reassertion of the view that divine inspiration is to be understood primarily in terms of divine speaking and divine revelation'.[88] It has to be asked, however, whether Abraham's identification of inspiration with coping with life's troubles, building up a community, aiding the poor and preaching the gospel has not made the concept of inspiration so broad as to make it virtually useless. In Abraham's hands the concept seems to have become an all-embracing term for religious existence. Furthermore, according to Abraham God inspires through his actions, but the concept of divine action remains just as mysterious as the concept of inspiration. And why should it be significant now that certain individuals were inspired by events long ago?

Social conceptions of inspiration

Biblical criticism has revealed that many biblical writings that now bear the name of a single individual were produced over a long period of time and involved many different, unnamed individuals. One possible way of dealing with this and retaining the concept of inspiration is to extend it from the single individual traditionally associated with a writing to all those involved in its production. The problem with this, however, is that modern biblical scholarship gives good reasons for holding that the production of a sacred writing stems not so much from a series of authors but rather from the community of faith in which it was written; the sacred writing reproduces not

[88] Ibid., p. 72.

merely the words of an important religious figure but also the response of the community to these words. The situation is complicated still further by the fact that, even when specific individuals may have been responsible for particular writings, they may merely be setting down religious beliefs that are already present in the community of which they are members. In other words, it is very difficult to separate the words of a prophet, or Jesus, or an apostle, from both the response of people to those words and the response of those who recorded those words. In view of this fact, some scholars have moved away from understanding inspiration as centred on an inspired author or authors and hold that it is centred in the tradition of the community of faith.[89] As an example of this type of approach we shall examine the theory of inspiration of the American scholar Paul Achtemeier.

According to Achtemeier, the results of critical study of the Bible

> ought to make it clear that our contemporary understanding of the origins of our Scripture, Old and New Testaments alike, has rendered obsolete the model of inspiration which understands the production of each

[89] For Schleiermacher, 'the Holy Spirit [is] the common spirit of the Church, and hence the source of all spiritual gifts and good works', including the scriptures, which share, though not exclusively, in the spirit of Christianity as embodied by Christ and taught by him to the disciples. Friedrich Schleiermacher, *The Christian Faith*, ed. H. R. Mackintosh and J. S. Stewart (Edinburgh: T&T Clark, 1989), § 130.2, p. 598. Rahner argues that biblical inspiration is an intrinsic part of God's foundation of the Church. As he puts it, 'The inspiration of the Scriptures is but simply the causality of God in regard to the Church, inasmuch as it refers to that constitutive element of the Apostolic Church, which is the Bible.' Karl Rahner, *Inspiration in the Bible*, p. 51. See also James Barr, *Holy Scripture: Canon, Authority, Criticism* (Oxford: Clarendon Press, 1983), p. 27.

Biblical book to be the result of the inspired work of an inspired author.'[90]

On the basis of this and similar considerations, Achtemeier concludes that the prophetic model of inspiration, that is, 'the prophetic model of one person writing one book',[91] should be replaced with a new, more adequate model of inspiration. The model Achtemeier proposes is based on the interaction of three key components: 'tradition', 'situation', and 'respondent'.[92]

'Traditions', Achtemeier writes, 'guard those past events which give to the community its uniqueness, and they aid the community in shaping its life in accordance with those originating events.'[93] Consequently, 'Traditions are . . . not primarily concerned with historical fact so much as they are concerned with the significance of those past events for the present, and the promise they hold for the future.'[94] It is not inerrancy but the expression of the present and future relevance of past, foundational events that constitutes the inspiration of scripture:

> What makes those traditions inspired is not any such statistical accuracy, but their witness to the ongoing presence of God with a community that looks to a decisive act of that God as its constitutive origin. The extent to which traditions carry out their task of representing to the community the activity it must pursue and the shape it must assume in the light of the originating act of God is the extent to which they are inspired.[95]

[90] Achtemeier, *Inspiration of Scripture*, pp. 103–4.
[91] Ibid., p. 122.
[92] Ibid., p. 134.
[93] Ibid., p. 124.
[94] Ibid., p. 125.
[95] Ibid.

The second key component of Achtemeier's theory of inspiration is what he terms 'situation'.[96] When the community of faith finds itself in a new situation, it draws on its traditions as a means of understanding it. At the same time, this need to apply traditions results in their modification in order to fit the new situation. The community of faith, however, does not regard the new situation as the result of chance events but, interpreting it in the light of its traditions, understands it to be under the guidance of God. 'For that reason,' Achtemeier writes, 'new situations and the new interpretations of tradition they elicit are understood by Scripture to be further evidence of the care and providence of the living God',[97] for,

> If Israel and the church find the presence of God's Spirit in the primal event of their existence, and in the traditions that event summoned forth, they also find that presence in the new situations confronting them, and seek to follow the guidance of that Spirit in their reinterpretations of their traditions.[98]

It is in this dynamic interaction between tradition and situation that the inspiration of scripture lies:

> It is for that reason that the dynamic nature of the traditions contained in our Biblical writings point to their inspiration, and must be acknowledged as playing a key role in any attempt to understand the inspiration of Scripture. It is that very dynamic nature that points to the continuing guidance of

[96] Ibid., pp. 126–31.
[97] Ibid., p. 131.
[98] Ibid.

> God's Spirit in the times our Scripture was being formed.[99]

The third component of Achtemeier's theory is what he terms the 'respondent', which he defines as 'anyone who contributes to the formulation and reformulation of tradition in specific situations'.[100] The respondent is thus the link between tradition and situation and the means by which they are brought together in a creative and dynamic relationship. But 'respondent', Achtemeier stresses, means much more than merely the individual responsible for the final, 'canonical' form of a biblical writing; it designates anyone who has contributed to the formation of a biblical writing. Thus, to take one of Achtemeier's examples,

> Not only the evangelist who gave the Gospel of Mark its final form can be thought of as respondent but those who first formulated the traditions about Jesus, who used and adapted them in their proclamation of the event of Christ, as well as those who began to assemble collections of similar stories, belong among the respondents who interpreted traditions in their situation and who have thus produced the inspired Scripture that we have.[101]

The advantages of this approach, Achtemeier claims, is that it does not really matter if most of the respondents are anonymous and, furthermore, 'we can also allow the proper role to the community of faith which played so large a part in the preservation and interpretation of traditions in new situations', for 'as the recipients and preservers of reinter-

[99] Ibid.
[100] Ibid., p. 132.
[101] Ibid., pp. 132–3.

preted traditions, they too played their role in the creation of our inspired Scriptures'.[102] Consequently, Achtemeier writes,

> It is not only the final assembler or compiler or author who shares in the inspiration which has produced Scripture. Rather, inspiration must be understood to be at work in all who have shaped, preserved, and assembled portions of the traditions contained in the several books.[103]

So 'inspiration must be seen in the long process by which the content, not only the final form, of the various Biblical books was produced'.[104] This means 'that the inspired nature of certain of those traditions [produced by Israel and the church] is an *a posteriori* discovery, not an *a priori* assumption',[105] because 'It was . . . from the interrelationship of tradition, situation, and respondent that the Holy Spirit summoned forth the words of Scripture.'[106]

There are, however, a number of problems with this approach. First, what sense does it make to speak of the Holy Spirit guiding the formation of the scriptures and simultaneously claim that inspiration is an a posteriori concept? Is it only in retrospect that we recognize the activity of the Spirit? Achtemeier provides no answer to this question.

A further problem is one that we have already frequently encountered in our discussion of non-verbal theories of inspiration, namely, what is the divine input in this understanding of inspiration? The danger is that, if the

[102] Ibid., p. 133.
[103] Ibid.
[104] Ibid., p. 135.
[105] Ibid.
[106] Ibid., p. 136.

composition of the Bible is understood as the result of the accumulation of a community's tradition, there seems to be little need to introduce God into the explanation. If this is the case, however, then the claim that the Bible is divinely inspired is undermined. Inspiration rests merely in the religious consciousness and insights of the community and not in God's interaction with his people.

Conclusion

The strengths of non-verbal theories of inspiration are above all their ability to do justice to the phenomena of scripture and their greater awareness of the subjective dimension of inspiration. The problem with non-verbal theories is that it is difficult to lay down clear criteria for establishing what in the Bible is due to God and what is due to the human author. One way of dealing with this problem is to use the state of human knowledge to evaluate the status of biblical material. Passages which modern scientific developments show to be mistaken should be regarded not as divine but as due to the influence of the contemporary culture and world-view. The problem with this is that human knowledge then comes to be given a higher status than the Bible and stands in judgement on the Bible's validity and credibility. This is a course of action that many Christians are not prepared to take. Furthermore, to discriminate between divine and human elements in the Bible means that not all of the Bible can be accepted as divinely inspired. The Bible as a *whole*, ceases to be a divine book.

Rejection of inspiration

In view of the numerous problems with the concept of inspiration, some scholars, such as John Barton, have doubted the usefulness of the concept.[107] Others have gone still further and advocated its abandonment altogether. This is the strategy advocated by R. P. C. Hanson, Roger Tomes and Gerd Lüdemann.

Hanson suggests that 'it would be more satisfactory and more honest if theologians gave up altogether using the words "inspired" and "inspiration" in connection with the Bible, and substituted for them another word, the word "unique"'.[108] For Hanson this uniqueness resides in the fact that 'the Bible is the supreme witness to the origins and significance of the Christian faith, the only primary, indispensable witness for it'.[109]

Like Hanson, Tomes sees the Bible as 'the indispensable source for our knowledge of those events on which we believe our relationship to God depends'.[110] He rejects the concept of inspiration, however, because, in his opinion, 'It is either too loaded or too vague to encompass what Christians have found in the Bible. It does not describe any feature of the text and therefore is not exegetically useful.'[111]

Lüdemann argues that the gulf between the historical facts of Jesus' life and the theological interpretation of these facts makes it impossible to sustain belief in the New Testament writings in any serious way or to equate the Word of God with the Holy Scriptures.[112] Furthermore, the claim that God addresses the reader in the scriptures is

[107] John Barton, *People of the Book? The Authority of the Bible in Christianity* (London: SPCK, 1988), p. 37.
[108] R. P. C. Hanson, *The Attractiveness of God* (London: SPCK, 1973), p. 14.
[109] Ibid., p. 15.
[110] Roger Tomes, 'Do we need a doctrine of inspiration?', *Theology Themes*, vol. 3, no. 2 (Spring 1995), 18–22; 21.
[111] Ibid., p. 22.
[112] Gerd Lüdemann, *Das Unheilige in der heiligen Schrift: Die andere Seite der Bibel* (Stuttgart: Radius, 1996), p. 12.

based on the questionable assumptions that God determined the canon and that the authors of the biblical writings were acting under God's orders. Study of the formation of the canon will reveal, however, the heavy hand of human involvement. In a collection of texts that so clearly bears the marks of human interference, Lüdemann asks, what sense does it make to speak of the Bible being inspired by God?

Another objection raised by Lüdemann concerns the claim that the biblical authors were commissioned by God. What grounds do we have for accepting that the authors of the biblical texts were acting under God's orders? The prophets may well have *believed* that God had spoken to them, but this was merely their own interpretation of their religious experience and we have no way of knowing whether this was a correct interpretation.[113] Another problem, Lüdemann argues, is that the concept of inspiration is based on the assumption that the various authors of the Bible are addressing not only their contemporaries but also those who would later read their writings. This presupposes that the meaning of the Bible then and now is identical, a presupposition that is untenable in the light of the gulf that separates the present from the past. Lüdemann concludes that

> It is therefore high time that we understood the Bible as a human work, awoke it out of its slumbers, and completely removed the monopoly that the Christian churches and large sections of so-called academic theology have successfully enforced in their highly selective interpretation of the Bible.[114]

[113] Ibid., p. 24.
[114] Ibid., p. 33.

Should we follow Hanson, Tomes and Lüdemann and abandon the concept of inspiration? There are a number of arguments that can be advanced against this course of action. If we wish to justify our commitment to a unique book, we must find a better reason than merely appealing to uniqueness, which is far too vague to be able to do the job Hanson requires of it. Hanson is clearly aware of this and grounds the uniqueness of the Bible on the fact that it is the unique witness to the events that gave rise to Christianity. At first sight, this might appear to be a helpful way of avoiding the problems associated with inspiration. A closer examination of this shift from inspiration to the concept of unique witness will reveal, however, that it too presents severe difficulties. The fundamental problem is: why should we accept the events witnessed to in the biblical texts as decisive for and determinative of our religious existence? The answer is that the witnesses to these events believed God to be present or active in them in some way. This divine presence or activity, however, does not seem to have been objectively observable by all those present. To take the most obvious example, not everyone responded to Jesus with faith, as the behaviour of the Pharisees makes abundantly clear. There is a good reason for this. As Kierkegaard has suggested in *Philosophical Fragments* and *Practice in Christianity*,[115] Jesus' status as Messiah or, as Kierkegaard prefers to put it, the God-man or the Eternal-in-time, was not immediately and empirically observable to his contemporaries but was concealed behind the incognito of his humanity. Christ's divinity was visible only to the eyes of faith. In other words, the witness of the

[115] Søren Kierkegaard, *Philosophical Fragments / Johannes Climacus*, ed. and trans. Howard V. Hong and Edna H. Hong (Princeton, NJ: Princeton University Press, 1985), pp. 30–5; *Practice in Christianity*, ed. and trans. Howard V. Hong and Edna H. Hong (Princeton, NJ: Princeton University Press, 1991), pp. 127–33.

New Testament is not a neutral assessment of the events that gave rise to Christianity but a record written from the perspective of faith. But what was it that prompted the New Testament writers to see the events concerning Jesus from the perspective of faith, while others were not drawn understand him in this way? This is the question that has to be addressed by those who wish to substitute the concept of unique witness for that of inspiration, for it is difficult to find a better answer than that the biblical writers were *inspired* to see God's hand in the events concerning Jesus. In other words, emphasis on the Bible as witness merely shifts our attention a stage further back from the texts themselves to the events and experiences that prompted the writing of these texts, begging the question: What is it about these events that makes them so significant?

Let us now turn to Tomes' claim that the concept of inspiration 'does not describe any feature of the text and therefore is not exegetically useful'.[116] Tomes is certainly right in his claim that there is no specific element in the text that we can identify as inspiration. But this is a trivial point, arising, in my opinion, from a failure to understand the nature, function and purpose of the concept of inspiration. Inspiration is a concept that concerns the spiritual rather than the scholarly use of the scriptures. To claim that the Bible is inspired is to claim that it is spiritually and existentially significant, that it has or should have a transforming impact upon the life of its reader. For someone to claim that the Bible is inspired is to state that he or she has encountered God in or by means of its pages, and that this collection of writings has become religiously definitive for, and determinative of, his or her existence. 'Inspiration' thus does not describe a specific feature of the text but indicates rather how the reader

[116] Tomes, 'Do we need a doctrine of inspiration?', p. 22.

should handle the Bible. It articulates the insight that the appropriate relation to the Bible on the part of the human being is submission to the Word of God which the Bible mediates.

The second element of Tomes' claim is that the concept of inspiration is not exegetically useful. The response we give to this claim will depend on whether we are approaching the Bible religiously or historically or, to put it another way, whether we approach the Bible as holy scripture or merely as a document worthy of scholarly study. If biblical exegesis is understood as descriptive historical analysis, as Tomes would seem to have us believe, then quite clearly there can be no place for inspiration, for it can shed little light on the historical processes which led to the formation of the biblical texts. However, while not wishing to deprecate the value of critical biblical scholarship, we must not forget that it is only *one* possible way of reading the Bible and, in my opinion, not even the most important way. In the quest for an understanding of the text, biblical scholarship sometimes seems to overlook the fundamental concern of the texts with which they are dealing: the human being's relationship with God. As Kenneth Leech puts it, in much modern scholarship 'we see a meticulous study of the text combined with an utter incapacity to be challenged by the Word'.[117] This is not to disparage biblical scholarship, but to call for it to be grounded in a concept that makes possible the *theological* exploitation of that scholarship (as opposed to purely historical or textual use).

It is on this basis that an argument can be advanced that the concept of inspiration is not merely exegetically useful but exegetically essential. The concept of inspiration underlies the *spiritual* exegesis of the Bible, that is, the

[117] Kenneth Leech, *Spirituality and Pastoral Care* (London: Sheldon, 1986), p. 7.

reading of the Bible as a spiritual book that is binding upon the existence of the human being. In this sense, inspiration is a theologically essential concept. This does not mean that faith is an essential requisite for interpreting the Bible, but that we should recognize, as Stuhlmacher puts it, that 'the biblical texts invite [the reader] to the confession and the living out of the faith'.[118] We do justice to the biblical texts only when we approach them with an openness to this invitation. It is not an invitation we are bound to accept, but one of which we should at least be conscious.

There are a number of responses that can be made to Lüdemann. Human involvement in the production of the biblical texts and their formation into a definitive canon does not of itself rule out some sort of divine guidance, difficult though it is to identify it precisely. With regard to the other points Lüdemann makes, we can respond that it is not of decisive importance whether the biblical writers believed they had received a communication from God or not. Nor is the gulf between the present and the past decisive. What is significant for our acceptance of the Bible as the divinely inspired Word of God is the impact of the biblical texts on us here and now. Can these texts, despite their human origins and problematic material, mediate to us a sense of the presence of God? Can they create a framework within which a divine–human encounter can take place?

The search for new models of inspiration

Should the difficulties associated with the various theories we have examined prompt us to abandon the attempt to

[118] P. Stuhlmacher, *Vom Verstehen des Neuen Testaments: Eine Hermeneutik* (Göttingen: Vandenhoeck & Ruprecht, 1979), pp. 219–20.

defend the authoritative position of the Bible? The answer to this question must surely be 'no' for two reasons. First, abandoning the concept of biblical authority fails to appreciate the role of the Holy Spirit in the acceptance of the Bible as authoritative. To approach the question of the Bible's significance from purely rational considerations is to ignore an essential feature of the claims made on behalf of the Bible, namely that acceptance of it as being from God is itself due to divine initiative and is not the result of an allegedly objective assessment of the biblical text.

Secondly, without some theory, no matter how flawed, to establish its centrality and pre-eminence over other works, the Bible's status as a source and norm of Christian theology is undermined. Despite the difficulties, then, theologians must continue to search for ways of articulating and justifying the authority of the Bible not just for those within the community of faith but also for those outside the Christian circle.

An alternative to abandoning the concept of inspiration is to search for more adequate models to express it. This is by far the more difficult of the two options open to us, for our study of word-centred and non-verbal theories of inspiration has revealed that none is free of difficulties. Such is the importance of the Bible for Christianity, however, that some defence of its authority must be undertaken. The traditional, and in my view most suitable, vehicle for this defence is the concept of inspiration, despite all the difficulties associated with it.

It is above all the supreme difficulty of showing the existence of a relationship between God and the Bible that makes the concept of inspiration so problematic. There are obvious and very powerful reasons for this difficulty. The question of God's relationship to the Bible can be seen as part of the more general theological problem of God's relationship to the world. How does God manifest himself in the world, if at all? And, assuming he does manifest himself, how do we recognize and identify this self-manifestation? What are the marks of God's presence? To answer these questions definitively and objectively we would have to be able to adopt an objective standpoint. We would have to be able to observe God and his relations to the world from 'outside', as it were, which is clearly impossible for beings who find themselves situated within the world. We are thus forced to treat God's relationship to the universe from the limited perspective imposed upon us by our status as finite, temporal entities, a perspective which means that we can never definitively and objectively answer the question of how God is related to the world.

The same problem applies to the question of God's relationship to the Bible, which can be seen as part of the general problem of God's relation to the world. To answer fully and definitively the question of God's relation to the biblical texts and their authors, we would have to be able to observe God's relation to the Bible from an objective standpoint, which is simply impossible for the human being. The problem with many theories of inspiration, and with those who reject the concept of inspiration altogether, is that they treat the Bible from this objective standpoint, as if it were an expression of what God is in himself, failing to recognize that it is only an expression of what God is *for us*.

One of the crucial questions that we must address if we are to be able to speak meaningfully of the divine inspiration of the Bible thus seems to be unanswerable. But there is a way out of this impasse and it is provided by taking the finite and temporal circumstances of human existence seriously. The impossibility of an objective approach to the question of inspiration means that we must take subjectivity as our starting-point. This does not mean that objective claims concerning the Bible are to be given up. It means that the objective question of inspiration, namely God's relationship to the Bible, can be answered only by viewing the question through the prism of human subjectivity. As we shall go on to see, it is precisely the consideration of inspiration from the perspective of human subjectivity that will enable us to gain some understanding of how God is related to the Bible and allow us to speak, albeit in a qualified sense, of the divine inspiration of scripture.

Although it is the relationship between God and the Bible that has tended to occupy the minds of most writers on biblical inspiration, I thus propose to take the *reader's* relationship to the biblical writings as the starting-point for the construction of a theology of inspiration. What does it mean for the reader to be inspired and what light does this throw on the texts by which he or she is inspired? Thus in the twofold relation that constitutes inspiration, namely God's relation to the Bible and the reader's relationship to the Bible, we shall take the latter as our starting-point and attempt to work back, as far as possible, to the former. In the pursuit of these aims I shall make extensive use of the thought of the German philosopher Karl Jaspers. Jaspers' philosophy provides useful resources for interpreting the nature of the reader's relation to the text. Above all, his concept of 'ciphers' provides a useful vehicle for considering in what sense the Bible can be said to be inspired.

4

The inspiration of the Bible

In our discussion of authority we saw that any authority the Bible might possess can only be epistemic and exemplary in nature. However, this epistemic and exemplary authority is of a special kind. First, although the Bible may provide knowledge about the history of early Israel, the origins of Christianity and the religious practices of ancient Judaism and early Christianity, this type of knowledge – historical knowledge – is not of paramount importance in the Bible and to the many individuals who contributed to its composition. First and foremost, the biblical writings articulate faith and their writers were moved to write by the impulse to communicate this faith to others. For Christian believers today, living long after the events that gave rise to the faith that motivated the biblical writers to compose their texts, the biblical texts are above all mediators of faith. Their epistemic content consists in the witness to what was believed to be the reality and action of God, and in insights into the nature of the divine–human relationship. It is from this that the exemplary authority of the Bible stems. The Bible possesses exemplary authority in so far as it provides examples and patterns for the human being's relationship with God. The problem is that of grounding this authority. What are the grounds for accepting the Bible as authoritative? We saw that there have been three traditional answers to this question, namely, that the Bible is divine revelation, that the Bible is the Word of God, and that the Bible is inspired. Because it has a more pronounced subjective dimension than the concepts of revelation and Divine Word, we suggested that 'inspiration' is the most appropriate and useful foundation upon which to construct a defence of the authoritative status of the Bible, for it is able to articulate not only the nature of the contents of the Bible but also the reader's response to the Bible.

In the two previous chapters we saw that theories of inspiration can be divided into two basic types, which have been described as 'conservative' and 'deductive', and 'liberal' and 'inductive' respectively. Our preferred designation of these two divisions, however, is 'word-centred' and 'non-verbal' theories, a designation which is aimed at expressing the view that conservative–deductive theories situate inspiration in the very words of the Bible, whereas the liberal–inductive approach understands inspiration as residing in the underlying message of the biblical text or in the processes which brought the biblical texts into existence. The strength of the word-based approach is its respect for the text and its consequent ability to apply inspiration to the whole of the Bible. Its weakness is its inability to deal adequately with the problematic material in the text, which it goes to unacceptable and implausible lengths to explain away. The word-centred approach seems to commit the believer to accepting as divine revelation material that seems at best dubious and at worst mistaken and even immoral. By focusing too excessively on the words of the text, the message that the authors of the text wish to mediate is in danger of being obscured.

The strength of the non-verbal approaches, on the other hand, is that they recognize that it is the spiritual content mediated by the words that is of paramount importance. The words are not significant in themselves, but only in so far as they mediate a spiritual message to human beings. This allows non-verbal approaches to deal with the problematic material in the Bible more easily than word-centred conceptions of inspiration. Such material is due to the human fallibility of the biblical writers and the historical and cultural conditions in which they were writing. Such material, however, does not detract from the basic message underlying the biblical text.

It is precisely the strength of the non-verbal approach to inspiration that constitutes its weakness, however, for the result of situating inspiration in an underlying message would seem to be that the text as such loses importance. The words are merely the vehicles for the biblical message, but the message as such is not dependent on these specific words and today there may well be more appropriate ways of expressing the content of the biblical message. This has the corollary that it is not the whole of the Bible that is inspired but only the 'message-bearing' parts of it. It thus becomes difficult to affirm that the Bible as a whole is inspired.

Is there any way of holding together the insights of both word-centred and message-centred approaches without falling prey to their weaknesses? Such a solution may be forthcoming if we take the interaction between reader and text as our starting-point. Much of the vagueness of writing about inspiration stems from taking the inspiration of the biblical *writers* as its starting-point. If we take the writer as our starting-point and consider, as Farrer suggests, 'how the minds of the sacred writers are moved as they write, in their passages of high inspiration',[1] then the comprehension of inspiration becomes an impossible task, for we are unable to gain access to the relationship that underlies the biblical writers' impulse to preach and/or write. Their God-

[1] Farrer, *Glass of Vision*, p. 56.

relationship is not at our disposal and we are consequently unable to ascertain why and how this relationship prompted them to communicate their experience of and insight into the will of God to their fellow human beings. The 'mechanism' involved in the communication of the divine will to the biblical writers is quite simply obscure to us. As Richard Smith rightly points out,

> the psychology of the human writer under the influence of inspiration escapes us, and probably always will. In itself the process of composing a written document is an obscure one; and under the influence of inspiration, that process can only be more obscure.[2]

Some of these problems and some of the vagueness of the concept of inspiration may be reduced if we focus not on the writer but on the impact of the biblical texts on the *reader*. Although we do not have access to the minds of the inspired writers and the God-relationship that allegedly prompts them to write, we do have access to the products of those inspired minds, namely the biblical texts. Furthermore, we also have access to how we ourselves react to and interact with these texts. A more appropriate starting-point, therefore, would seem to be the impact of the biblical text upon the reader.

A further justification for taking the reader as our starting-point for the construction of a theology of inspiration is the presence in the biblical texts of what Körtner has

[2] Richard J. Smith, 'Inspiration and inerrancy', in Raymond E. Brown, Joseph A. Fitzmyer, Roland E. Murphy, *The Jerome Biblical Commentary*, 2 vols (London: Geoffrey Chapman, 1968), vol. 2, pp. 499–514; 509, § 55.

aptly termed 'the implicit reader'.[3] The production of any text implies at least the possibility that it will be read. The consigning of anything to paper thus implies the presence of a reader. Indeed, the presence of the reader is essential for the 'completion' of the text, for the act of reading is the means by which the meaning and significance of the text is actualized in the present. This does not mean, however, that the reader imposes an alien meaning upon the text, or is free to interpret the text in any way he or she thinks fit. The hermeneutical task is that of understanding oneself before the text and allowing oneself to be formed and reformed by the text. As Körtner puts it, 'In the act of reading the reader gets involved with the text in order thereby to bring the text to completion and at the same time to allow him or herself to be reconstituted as a subject.'[4] Text and reader exist in a dialectical relationship in which the meaning of the text is constituted anew by the reader and the reader is reconstituted as a subject through the act of reading.

The reader implied by the biblical texts is, as Körtner points out, the *inspired* reader: 'The reader *implied* by the biblical texts is a reader *inspired* by the Spirit of God.'[5] He goes on to comment:

> The meaning of the biblical texts constitutes itself anew in such acts of reading in which the reader of these texts learns to understand him or herself in a new way, which the language of Christian tradition describes as faith. The problem of inspiration thus returns to theological debate, but shifts from the text

[3] Ulrich H. J. Körtner, *Der inspirierte Leser: Zentrale Aspekte biblischer Hermeneutik* (Göttingen: Vandenhoeck & Ruprecht, 1994), p. 16.
[4] Ibid., p. 60.
[5] Ibid., p. 16.

or its author to the reader and the act of reading.'[6]

That is, the reader's role in the construction of textual meaning in reading the Bible entails the return of the concept of inspiration, but now inspiration is situated primarily in the *reader*.

This centring of inspiration in the reader should not, however, take us down the postmodernist road of the 'death of the author'[7] and the decentring or indeed destruction of the human subject.[8] The postmodernist view that literary creativity arises from immanent factors within the act and process of writing constitutes a hypostatizing and absolutizing of language which eliminates the referential function of the text. Literature becomes understood as a radically finite performative whose existence is exhausted in its speaking and writing.[9] There is nothing beyond it to which it points. It is in and for itself. The text's mediatory, transcendental function as it appears in both Greco-Roman and Christian conceptions of inspiration is negated and replaced by a deification of the contingency and finitude of the signifier.[10]

[6] Ibid.

[7] See above all Roland Barthes, 'The death of the author', in *Image, Music, Text*, essays selected and translated by Stephen Heath (London: Fontana, 1977), pp. 142–8. For a study and critique of the notion of the 'death of the author' see Seán Burke, *The Death and Return of the Author: Criticism and Subjectivity in Barthes, Foucault and Derrida* (Edinburgh: Edinburgh University Press, 2nd edn., 1998).

[8] See, for example, Roland Barthes, *Sade / Fourier / Loyola*, trans. Richard Miller (New York: Hill and Wang, 1976), pp. 8–9; Michel Foucault, *The Order of Things: An Archaeology of the Human Sciences* (London: Tavistock, 1970), p. 386.

[9] See esp. Barthes, 'Death of the author', pp. 145–6.

[10] See Maurice Blanchot, *The Space of Literature*, trans. Ann Smock (Lincoln, NE: University of Nebraska Press, 1982), ch. V; Jacques Derrida, 'Che cos'è la poesia?', in Peggy Kamuf (ed.), *A Derrida*

The theology of inspiration is committed, however, to what postmodernist writers disparage as the 'theological' conception of the act of reading.[11] That is, the theology of inspiration is committed to the view that the text is not self-contained but points beyond itself to a reality which, though mediated by the text, it nevertheless independent of it. For the believer the divine 'author' of the biblical texts can never be reduced to a fiction emanating from the immanent processes involved in the act of writing.

The problem faced by theologies of inspiration is not the death of the (divine) author but his elusiveness and the inaccessibility of his relationship to the human beings and texts he inspires. It is this that compels us to take the reader as the basis for considering in what sense the biblical texts can be said to be inspired. If we can gain some insight into how the biblical texts impact on the reader, then we may have a basis for constructing a theology of inspiration that is not dependent upon the impossible task of isolating the mechanism(s) by which God inspired the biblical writers.

Such a starting-point in the reader will not eliminate all of the problems associated with inspiration. Inspiration will always remain an elusive concept irrespective of our starting-point, precisely because we stand within the divine–human relationship and are thus unable to observe it 'objectively' from some neutral standpoint. For this reason the Bible and the ciphers it contains are not compelling. There is no external, objective standard by which we can judge the degree to which an individual or text is inspired. There is always a significant personal involvement in the question of inspiration which means

Reader: Between the Blinds (London: Harvester Wheatsheaf, 1991), pp. 221–37; Timothy Clark, *Theory of Inspiration*, esp. chs 10 and 11.

[11] See Barthes, 'Death of the author', p. 146.

that we shall never be able to provide a watertight, utterly compelling exposition, justification, or defence of inspiration.[12] We can, however, sketch the potential impact that the biblical texts may have on the reader, if the reader permits them to do so. Whether the reader experiences such an impact will depend, however, upon the degree to which he or she is prepared to engage with the Bible and be addressed by it. In the language adopted in this study, it may be possible to construct a theology of inspiration by examining first the nature of human being and its relation to Transcendence and then consider how texts are able to mediate Transcendence and have an impact on human being. We can construct a theology of inspiration by attempting to articulate how decisive the Bible is or can be for human existence. By 'existence' here we mean qualitative or authentic existence. That is, a defence of the inspired status of the Bible can be constructed by focusing on and articulating the way these texts impact on the human being and open up possibilities for a qualitatively higher mode of existence. We can express this in another way: the inspired status of the Bible can be defended if we can show that it can contribute to human self-transcendence. The question of the Bible's inspiration is most

[12] This is not, however, an argument for the abandonment of inspiration. It is precisely at the deepest levels of human being that the greatest mismatch occurs between what we wish to say and the materials we have for saying it. Human love is a good example. It is arguably impossible to provide objectively compelling reasons to persuade a sceptic that I love and am loved by another human being. I may be able to point to certain phenomena which I regard as indicative of the existence of a love relationship, such as duration, intimacy, a sense of security and so on, but a sceptic will always be able to provide plausible alternative explanations – biological, psychological, economic – for these phenomena. Such reductionist explanations of the love relationship will, however, fail to convince anyone who has experienced such a relationship.

profitably addressed by posing it in the context of human existence and the concrete existential issues arising from the human condition. In the following we shall draw on existentialist accounts of human existence, particularly that of Karl Jaspers, in our attempt to situate biblical inspiration in the reader's engagement with the biblical texts.

Now the construction of a theology of inspiration from a starting-point in human existence is clearly in need of some justification. Two criticisms immediately spring to mind. First, such an approach requires the development of an anthropology and would thus seem to be dependent upon an essentialist view of human selfhood as a conglomeration of 'givens' or fixed properties. To speak in terms of a stable human self, it could be argued, is to fail to recognize the particularity, contingency and historicity of human beings. The human self is a social construct arising from the societal, political and cultural forces at work in the context in which the human being finds him or herself. There is thus no core nature common to all human beings which remains unchanged over the generations. If there is no such thing as human nature, then clearly an attempt to construct a theology of inspiration on the basis of an understanding of human existence would be doomed to failure.

The anti-essentialist critique, however, is applicable only to static conceptions of human nature and the force of its argument can be met if we conceive of human nature more loosely and dynamically than has often been the case. We should not abandon the concept of human nature but rather sever the connection between nature and fixity, understanding human selfhood as dynamic, open and self-transcending. This would entail our understanding human selfhood in terms of *task*. This task, which is both particular and unique to each one of us and also universal in the sense that all human beings are faced by it, is to synthesize the given structure of the self into a coherent whole.

A second indicator of the reality of a common, albeit dynamic and fragmentary, human nature is the universal human experience of boundary situations such as anxiety, guilt, despair and the threat of death. These crises are universal. It is therefore possible to give an abstract, 'essentialist' account of them. At the same time, however, each individual experiences these existential crises as unique to him or herself. Each human being is a unique, irreplaceable individual and the self he or she constructs in the light of the experience of existential crisis will be a self that is unique to that human being. We can thus agree with Macquarrie when he writes:

> In general we may say that the question about a 'nature' in man must be answered negatively if nature is conceived in either static or subhuman terms, but it may be answered affirmatively if one has developed a sufficiently dynamic conception of nature, appropriate to the human existent.[13]

A theology of inspiration which takes as its starting-point the reader of the biblical texts is not undermined by the anti-essentialist critique if it adopts a dynamic conception of human selfhood.

Another possible objection to an existential approach to inspiration is that it is illegitimate to apply to the Bible concepts drawn from outside the biblical thought-world. To apply concepts derived from existential philosophy to the Bible, it might be claimed, is to make non-biblical ideas the criteria by which the biblical texts are judged, thus setting

[13] John Macquarrie, *Existentialism* (Harmondsworth: Penguin, 1973), p. 71.

such ideas above the Bible. In response to this we might point out that certain passages in the Bible seem to provide a basis for our existential approach. Thus in the Gospel of John we find written: 'he who does what is true comes to the light' (John 3.21). This and similar biblical passages (see, e.g., John 8.32; 18.37) make clear, as Forrester points out, that 'The truth is not regarded as something to be contemplated or examined in a detached way; it is to be encountered, lived out, related to, but above all *loved* if it is to be truly known.'[14] That is, the Bible is not concerned with information but with truth, not with knowing but with being. The religious seeker reads the Bible not because he or she wishes to *know* more but because he or she believes that through reading the Bible and appropriating its insights, possibilities for fuller, more authentic human *being* may be uncovered. As we saw in our discussion in chapter 2, there is little overt reference in the Bible to verbal inspiration, inerrancy and so on. There does seem, however, to be a great deal in the Bible that pertains to matters that are decisive for human existence. In applying existential concepts to the Bible, then, we are not imposing an alien framework upon it but are merely drawing out ideas already present, indeed ideas which are fundamental to much of the Bible's teaching.

A second response to the claim that by starting with human existence we are imposing alien categories on the Bible is to draw attention to the insight that knowledge of God involves knowledge of self. Accepting God involves far more than simply accepting that the term 'God' has an objective reference; i.e., that 'God' maps on to an objective reality. Understanding the concept of God involves acquir-

[14] Duncan B. Forrester, 'Practical Theology', in Paul Avis (ed.), *The Threshold of Theology* (Basingstoke: Marshall Pickering, 1988), pp. 125–39; 125, original emphasis.

ing a knowledge of how this term impacts upon one's existence. As Charles Wood puts it,

> The knowledge of God . . . is not, in the first instance, to be thought of as information about God which it is in one's interest to possess. To use the familiar distinction, it is not 'knowledge about' but 'knowledge of' . . . It is a sustained personal awareness or existential apprehension of God, which profoundly determines one's existence.[15]

This determination of one's existence does not come about as the direct result of knowledge of God, however. It is a misunderstanding of the relationship between knowledge of God and knowledge of self to claim that once one has been provided with knowledge about God, then one begins to live in a new and different fashion on the grounds of this information. The relationship between knowledge of God and knowledge of self is dialectical in nature. The only way one can come to know God is through existential development, yet at the same time one's existential development is conditioned and given new impulses by one's knowledge of God. A useful analogy for understanding what is involved in the knowledge of God is our knowledge of other persons. In order to know another person, some development and emotional and intellectual growth is required on the part of the knower. The knower must have grasped to some extent such concepts as trust, respect, hope, value, joy, obligation, fidelity and so on, if personal knowledge of any depth is to come about. Without the command of such concepts, which can be acquired only through existential and personal growth, an individual's knowledge of another person will be

[15] Charles M. Wood, *The Formation of Christian Understanding: An Essay in Theological Hermeneutics* (Philadelphia: Westminster, 1981), p. 32.

very superficial indeed. But the situation is still more complex than I have described it thus far, for our knowledge of existential concepts such as trust, etc., comes about through our interaction with other persons. That is, it is through our interaction with other persons that we acquire the basis for our knowledge of other persons. It is through our interaction with others that we learn the meaning of such terms as trust, respect, hope, value, joy, obligation and fidelity.

Thus one justification for an existential approach to biblical authority is that many central Christian concepts have existential presuppositions or require some existential grounding before they can be understood. That is, the comprehension and acceptance of Christian concepts frequently requires a prior moral and emotional development before these concepts can be appropriated. For example, the concept of thanksgiving becomes intelligible and able to be appropriated only when the individual has previously acquired some understanding of gratitude in a human context. As Wood points out, 'to learn these characteristically Christian concepts, and thus to "understand Christianity", involves one in what may be a fairly intensive and thoroughgoing education in human existence'.[16] We are not born with such concepts as faith, hope and love; they have to be learnt. Wood comments:

> Theologically understood, faith, hope, and love are divine gifts, not to be reckoned as human achievements; yet the appropriation of these gifts, enabled by grace, just as clearly involves the development of the corresponding abilities, or clusters of abilities, which are then determinative of Christian life as lived 'in the power of the Holy Spirit'.[17]

[16] Ibid., p. 25.
[17] Ibid.

Similarly, many of the central doctrines of the Christian faith are more than merely intellectual propositions and require existential appropriation on the part of the believer if they are to be fully grasped. Wood points out that 'the concepts involved in, say, "creation", "incarnation", and "resurrection" are not simply elements of a Christian hypothesis or world view but are ingredient in Christian life itself'.[18] The understanding of such concepts involves not merely grasping their conceptual content, but allowing them to transform one's existence.[19]

The nature of human existence

The fundamental meaning of the term 'existence' is 'given, factual, empirical, concrete reality'. That is, to say of something that it 'exists' is to claim that this 'something' is to be found somewhere in the world. Human beings have factual existence, for they too are given, concrete, empirical realities. When used of human beings in the sense of factual existence, 'existence' refers to the brute facticity of human existence. Existence in this sense is the necessary condition for our being in the world and furthermore, Jaspers tells us, is 'the reality which everything must enter so as to be real for us'.[20]

The type of existence with which we are concerned here, however, is what has been variously described as 'qualitative' or 'authentic' existence. The term usually employed to designate this qualitatively different type of existence is *Existenz*. It is helpful, however, if we differentiate still

[18] Ibid.
[19] Ibid., p. 26.
[20] Karl Jaspers, *Philosophical Faith and Revelation*, trans. E. B. Ashton (London: Collins, 1967), p. 63.

further. Some of the problems associated with existential philosophy arise from a failure to distinguish between the given existential structure of the human being and the self that that human being constructs through the creative choices he or she makes on the basis of this given existential structure. To facilitate our discussion of human existence we thus distinguish between two types, or rather levels, of human existence, namely 'structural' and 'authentic' existence. By structural existence we mean the given structure of human existence, those qualities the human being possesses which constitute his or her personhood. Older forms of philosophy would have designated this type of existence human nature or essence. If nature or essence is understood as the properties a thing must possess in order to be the thing that it is, then structural existence can indeed be understood as a form of essence or nature. However, it must be stressed that the essence or nature that is structural existence does not consist of fixed properties, but is above all a series of possibilities. Structural existence comprises those possibilities that constitute the human being, which, if brought together adequately, result in the positing of a coherent self and the achievement of authentic existence.

The human being can be said to comprise a series of dipolar opposites. Kierkegaard describes the self as a synthesis or relation of body and mind, the temporal and the eternal, the infinite and the finite, and freedom and necessity.[21] Macquarrie, on the other hand, understands human existence to comprise the following polarities:

[21] Søren Kierkegaard, *Concept of Anxiety*, ed. and trans. with introduction and notes by Reidar Thomte in collaboration with Albert B. Anderson (Princeton, NJ: Princeton University Press, 1980), pp. 43, 88, 90–1; *Sickness unto Death*, ed. and trans. Howard V. Hong and Edna H. Hong (Princeton, NJ: Princeton University Press, 1980), pp. 13–14.

possibility–facticity; rationality–irrationality; responsibility–impotence; anxiety–hope; individual–society.[22] The most fundamental and significant of these is the possibility–facticity polarity, under which all the other polarities can be subsumed.

The human self, then, is fundamentally ambiguous. It is not a homogeneity but a complex juxtaposition of interacting elements. The fundamental question confronting each human being is that of finding some way to bring the disparate elements of the self together into a coherent whole. The task facing the self is complicated still further by the fact that the human self is finite and contingent. We are thrown into existence, as Heidegger puts it,[23] and our being is constantly threatened by, and ultimately ends in, death. Ours is a 'being-towards-death',[24] a being which is permeated and, it would seem, ultimately overwhelmed by non-being.

There are two possible ways for the human being to address the problem of the ambiguity and finitude of human existence, namely the atheistic and the theistic. Both approaches have in common an awareness of the finitude and contingency of human existence and the fact that human existence is not self-sufficient: the human being is not naturally in possession of the resources that would give his or her life meaning, purpose and significance. Both approaches also realize that acceptance of facticity means, among other things, accepting our lack of wholeness and our incapacity to achieve existential wholeness by means of our own powers. The atheistic position, however, maintains that this is the whole picture. It is a

[22] John Macquarrie, *Principles of Christian Theology* (London: SCM Press, 1977), pp. 62–8.
[23] Martin Heidegger, *Being and Time*, trans. John Macquarrie and Edward Robinson (Oxford: Blackwell, 1962), p. 174.
[24] Ibid., pp. 279–311.

position that has famously been adopted by Sartre, who holds that, since there is no God, there are no resources outside the self which the self can use. Consequently, Sartre argues, there is no resolution of the ambiguities of human existence. On the contrary, the polarities and contradictions of human life render it absurd and meaningless. 'Man', he concludes, 'is a useless passion.'[25]

The other approach to the ambiguity and finitude of human existence is to understand the ambivalent structure of the human self as indicating the possibility of a deeper level at which these ambiguities and contradictions are resolved. In Macquarrie's words,

> we look for a further dimension in the situation, a depth beyond both man and nature that is open to us in such a way that it can make sense of our finite existence by supporting it and bringing order and fulfillment into it.[26]

This lack of self-containedness means that human existence must be conceived of as having a 'transcendent' dimension. Human existence points beyond itself in the sense that it cannot find the focal point for its existence within itself. As Macquarrie puts it, 'selfhood is attained only in so far as the existent is prepared to look beyond the limits of his own self for the master concern that can create such a stable and unified self'.[27] Authentic selfhood can come about only when the human being is focused on something that lies outside the immanent structure of the self and is capable of imposing coherence and wholeness

[25] Jean-Paul Sartre, *Being and Nothingness. An Essay on Phenomenological Ontology*, trans. Hazel E. Barnes (New York: Philosophical Library, no date), p. 615.
[26] Macquarrie, *Principles of Christian Theology*, p. 73.
[27] Ibid., p. 79.

upon the self.

How, then, does the human being go about achieving this coherence? The first point we should make is that existential unity does not come about without effort on the part of each single individual. Each human being must engage in the quest for authentic selfhood with the appropriate existential disposition if he or she is to achieve existential unity. According to Macquarrie, the conditions for bringing about existential unity and achieving authentic selfhood are *commitment* and *acceptance*. 'Commitment,' he writes,

> is the prospective view of this unity, for it has to do with the future, with the possibilities of existence. A committed existence is one that has in view some master possibility. In consistently directing itself on this master possibility, the other possibilities of life are subordinated to it and the movement is toward unified selfhood. The absence of such a commitment results in an existence that jumps from one immediate possibility to the next, an existence that may be very much at the mercy of chance circumstances or changing desires and that has only the lowest degree of selfhood and unity.[28]

Acceptance, on the other hand,

> is the retrospective view of the self's unity, for it has to do with what has been, with the situation that already obtains and in which we find ourselves. If anything like unified selfhood is to be reached, the facticity of the situation has to be accepted in its entirety, with no loose ends rejected.[29]

[28] Ibid., p. 77.
[29] Ibid., pp. 77–8.

To attain authentic existence the human self has to be organized around some focal point or, as Macquarrie puts it, be committed to a master possibility. Such a focal point or master possibility provides the centre around which the disparate elements that comprise the self can be brought together into a coherent whole. We saw earlier that the theistic position is that such a focal point or master possibility does not belong to the human being's resources. The human being is thus compelled to look beyond him or herself for the source of existential unity.

Transcendent being

What, then, can give human existence meaning? The answer to this question is *Being*. Human being is finite, limited and contingent and so does not contain within itself the resources whereby it can adequately answer the questions its own being throws up. That which can give human existence meaning must thus be or possess that being which human being lacks. It is worth quoting Macquarrie at this point:

> What is it, then, that confronts us and reveals itself when we have become aware of the nothingness of ourselves and our world? The answer is: Being. It is against the foil of nothing that for the first time our eyes are opened to the wonder of being, and this happens with the force of revelation.[30]

The question of Being[31] is far more than merely a

[30] Ibid., 87.
[31] In order to distinguish Being from individual beings and from human being we have chosen to capitalize the term.

philosophical or metaphysical question. It is rooted in the question of our own being. This means that the fundamental question 'What is Being?' breaks down from the human perspective into two secondary questions, namely, 'What am I?' and 'What is my authentic purpose?'[32] The question of Being thus becomes the question of the meaning of Being for us. Being is that which human being lacks, whose appropriation or acquisition would provide human being with meaning.

What, then, is the nature of Being? Being is not to be identified with anything that is in the world. That is, it is not *a* being and cannot be identified with any reality, no matter how exalted, that is to be found within the universe. Being is not *a* being. Being is *sui generis*. Nor, as Macquarrie points out, can Being

> be equated with substance, the ὑποκεῖμενον or substratum sometimes supposed to underlie the phenomenal characteristics of beings. Leaving aside some of the other problems which the notion of 'substance' raises, it cannot be equated with 'being' because it is above all a static idea, having thinghood for its model.[33]

Furthermore, Being is not a property in the way shape, colour, and texture are properties of beings in the world. It is of a fundamentally different order from these properties. Indeed, it is the condition which makes shape, colour and texture possible. To say of something that it *is*, is to say something of a different order from saying that it is red, round and soft.

A further characteristic of Being is that it is not

[32] Cf. Karl Jaspers, *Philosophy*, 3 vols, trans. E. B. Ashton (Chicago: University of Chicago Press, 1969–71), vol. I, p. 1.
[33] Macquarrie, *Principles of Christian Theology*, p. 109.

conditioned by the subject–object dichotomy. Being can be neither subject nor object, for both imply a separation or differentiation of Being. To describe Being as subject would be to differentiate it from objects, which would mean that there would be something Being does not encompass, namely, objects. To understand Being as an object would be to differentiate it from the subject, which would again mean that there would be something Being does not encompass, namely, the subject. In other words, understandings of Being which are unable to transcend the subject–object dichotomy are unable to do justice to Being. Being lies at the basis of everything, both subject and object; therefore, if anything is excluded from a conception of Being, that conception cannot be adequate and cannot do justice to Being. The conclusion which we must draw from this is that Being cannot be understood in terms of the subject–object dichotomy.[34]

Finally, Being should not be understood as a class, not even as the broadest, most capacious class there is, the class which includes all things. This view is rejected by Aristotle, who writes: 'It is not possible that either unity or being should be a single genus of things.'[35] Heidegger makes a similar point, arguing that the universality of Being should not lead us to regard Being simply as a class or genus. Although Being is indeed universal, 'the "universality" of Being *"transcends"* any universality of genus'.[36] Later in *Being and Time*, Heidegger writes:

[34] For a discussion of the subject–object dichotomy, see Karl Jaspers, *Philosophy is for Everyman: A Short Course in Philosophical Thinking*, trans. R. F. C. Hull and Grete Wels (London: Hutchinson, 1967), pp. 22–3; *Way to Wisdom: An Introduction to Philosophy*, trans. Ralph Manheim (London: Victor Gollancz, 1951), pp. 28–38; *Philosophical Faith and Revelation*, p. 61.

[35] Aristotle, *Metaphysics*, 998[36b] p. 21.

[36] Heidegger, *Being and Time*, p. 22.

> Being, as the basic theme of philosophy, is no class or genus of entities; yet it pertains to every entity. Its 'universality' is to be sought higher up. Being and the structure of Being lie beyond every entity and every possible character which an entity may possess. *Being is the transcendens pure and simple.*[37]

In other words, Being should not be identified with a class of things, not even with the class of all things. It is not a collective term for all that there is in the world. Being goes beyond all that is in the world, even when all that is in the world is taken together as a collective unity. As such, Being transcends human thinking, despite all our attempts to think it. As Jaspers puts it, 'I can . . . neither conceive this absolute being nor give up trying to conceive it. This being is transcendence, because I cannot grasp it but must transcend to it in thoughts that are completed when I cannot think them.'[38] The most appropriate designation of Being, then, is that it is transcendent. Being is Transcendence – but what is Transcendence?

The question of Transcendence is not an abstract question, despite the abstractness of the term 'Transcendence'. Nor is the question of Transcendence a pseudo-question. The question of Transcendence forces itself upon our attention through the sheer facticity of our existence. This question is not removed simply by ignoring it or refusing to speak of it, for, as we saw earlier, it confronts us as a consequence of the contingency and finitude of human being. The way in which we raise and answer the question may vary, but the question of Transcendence remains, regardless of whether we are theists or atheists.

[37] Ibid., p. 62; original emphasis.
[38] Jaspers, *Philosophy*, III, p. 34.

Since Kant's 'transcendental turn', Transcendence has been reduced to a purely human activity, with no extra-mental or cosmological reference. The term has come to be used to describe the operations of the human consciousness. Transcendence in this sense describes a transcending that takes place in the subject's thinking. Such thinking is 'transcendental' in that it constitutes reflection on the possibilities and limitations of cognition. It is immanently epistemological.

Among the non-theistic existentialists such as Heidegger, Sartre and Merleau-Ponty this transcendental turn manifests itself as a consideration of the transcendence of human being within the contours of being-in-the-world. Transcendence is a possibility of Dasein and as such is a quality of the human subject with nothing beyond it. Transcendence in this sense is immanently existential.

For Jaspers, however, Transcendence is not swallowed up by subjectivity and cannot be exhausted by describing the self-transcending subject. Self-transcendence is not identical with the Being of Transcendence-itself, for this would reduce Transcendence and Being to aspects of human subjectivity. There is present in Transcendence an Otherness that is not reducible to human subjectivity, although subjectivity is the only means by which we can gain access to it. Transcendence is an objective reality but one which can never be grasped as an object. Olson comments:

> for Jaspers . . . the discovery that reason cannot operate as metaphysical realists once claimed does not put an end to metaphysics but only ontology. As in the case of Kierkegaard, the logical paradoxes of transcendental reflection point to a deeper reality through paradox whereby one apprehends a reality which can only be termed haltingly the 'Super-

> sensible' or Transcendence-Itself; a reality which is not known as an object but which beckons as 'cipher'. Ontology, then, is reconstituted as existential metaphysics.[39]

The term 'Transcendence', then, expresses the idea that human beings can grasp or be grasped by a reality that is not reducible to what is given in the world.

But what is the nature of Transcendence and how do we as human beings gain access to it? Here we are confronted by a seemingly insuperable problem, for we cannot describe Transcendence. As Jaspers puts it,

> Transcendence is not defined in categories; it does not exist as empirical reality; nor does it lie in the presence of my freedom as such. It is thus not in any of the modes of being that lend themselves to objectively articulated thought, or to cognition as existence which I have to take for granted, or to elucidation in an appeal to my potential.[40]

'The human being', Jaspers writes, 'cannot deal directly with hidden Transcendence.'[41] All attempts to think Transcendence by means of universal concepts are thus condemned to failure.

[39] Alan M. Olson, *Transcendence and Hermeneutics. An Interpretation of the Philosophy of Karl Jaspers* (The Hague: Martinus Nijhoff, 1979), p. 80.
[40] Jaspers, *Philosophy*, III, p. 7.
[41] Jaspers, *Philosophical Faith and Revelation*, p. 143.

Thinking about transcendent Being: the ciphers

If transcendent Being transcends the subject–object dichotomy and consequently cannot be thought, how can we acquire any comprehension of it and, still more importantly, sustain a relationship to it? The human being thinks in the categories of the general consciousness,[42] which is conditioned by the subject–object dichotomy. Indeed, the subject–object dichotomy is the 'basic condition of our thinking'.[43] It is the natural and unavoidable human tendency to see everything in terms of subject (ourselves) and object (that which is not ourselves). It is here that we are confronted with a major problem. If, as we saw earlier, Being is beyond the subject–object divide, how can we come to sustain any kind of relationship to it? Without participation in general consciousness and its concepts, thought is impossible, and yet because consciousness and the concepts it produces are conditioned by the subject–object dichotomy, that which lies beyond this dichotomy would seem literally to be unthinkable. Our attempts to think and speak of Being are not only inadequate, they are also a distortion of what Being truly is, for they impose a structure on Being, namely the subject–object dichotomy, that is inappropriate to the nature of Being. At the same time, however, it is absolutely essential to find some way of communicating the reality of Being and expressing that reality in human language. If it is impossible to find models, flawed though they might be, by means of which we can express our experience of Being, then Being becomes an inexpressible, incommunicable, private experience.

To put the problem of expressing Being in language in a different way, we could say that there is a mismatch

[42] Jaspers, *Philosophy*, I, pp. 54–6.
[43] Jaspers, *Way to Wisdom*, p. 29.

between language and Being because our language has developed as a means for talking about beings in the world. Consequently, it is ill-suited to describing what is not *a* being but Being as such, a reality which transcends all individual beings in the world.

How, then, can we know Being, which, as we have seen, is decisive for our existence and the attainment of authentic selfhood, without forcing Being into structures which distort its nature and meaning? In short, we are confronted by a severe epistemological problem, namely how can human beings come to know Being? As Jaspers puts it: 'The question is: What is Being? The question to this question is: how can I and how must I think of Being?'[44] Jaspers' answer to this question is to introduce the concept of *ciphers*.

The ciphers

The ciphers have two functions. First, they create or provide an avenue to Transcendence. 'Ciphers', Jaspers writes, 'are like a language of Transcendence.'[45] Since 'Transcendence itself does not become phenomenal at all', Jaspers tells us, 'the cipher language takes the place of its appearance.'[46] That is, ciphers are the means by which human beings can encounter Transcendence despite the transcendence of Transcendence. They are prisms of Transcendence formulated in the language of the subject–object dichotomy: 'The concepts, images, ideas in the medium of consciousness at large in which I, as possible Existenz, hear a transcendent language are called ciphers of Transcendence.'[47]

[44] Jaspers, *Von der Wahrheit* (Munich: Piper, 1947), p. 37.
[45] Jaspers, *Philosophy is for Everyman*, p. 93.
[46] Jaspers, *Philosophical Faith and Revelation*, p. 94.
[47] Ibid., p. 95.

Secondly, ciphers shed light on human existence and thereby facilitate the human being's journey towards authentic existence. These two functions are dialectically enmeshed with each other. It is precisely the fact that the ciphers constitute an avenue to Transcendence that gives them the power to impel the human being towards authentic existence. At the same time, it is only when the human being appropriates the ciphers that he or she can make progress towards authentic existence. This dialectical relationship between these two functions of ciphers is succinctly expressed by Jaspers as follows: 'The magnetism of Transcendence for Existenz is voiced in ciphers. They open areas of Being. They illuminate my decisions. They enhance or dampen my awareness of being, and of myself.'[48] Ciphers achieve this by pointing beyond the subject–object dichotomy to Transcendence. Ciphers, then, are not knowledge or cognition. Rather, they create a 'vision' of Transcendence.[49] To understand how ciphers achieve this, it is necessary to distinguish them from signs and symbols.

A sign is something which points beyond itself to another immediate reality. As Jaspers puts it: 'Signs designate another reality that can be directly expressed, seen, and known.'[50] Thus a traffic sign points beyond its own reality as a piece of metal shaped in a particular way to a feature of the road which lies before it. But the meaning of the traffic sign is exhausted in the reality to which it points. There is no 'surplus of meaning', as Ricoeur puts it. Signs are transparent, unambiguous and unproblematic.

Symbols have in common with signs the fact that they

[48] Ibid., p. 92.
[49] Ibid.
[50] Jaspers, *Der philosophische Glaube angesichts der Offenbarung* (Munich: Piper, 1962), p. 192 (my translation); *Philosophical Faith and Revelation*, p. 122.

too point beyond themselves. Ricoeur's distinction between signs and symbols is helpful here: 'Symbol is a sign in this, that like every sign it intends something beyond and stands for this something.' There are, however, several important differences between signs and symbols: 'But not every sign is a symbol. Symbol conceals in its intention a double intentionality. There is the first, the primary or literal intentionality, which, like any meaningful intentionality, implies the triumph of the conventional sign over the natural.' Then there is a 'second intentionality' which points beyond itself to a second meaning that transcends and is not encompassed by the primary or literal intentionality. As Ricoeur puts it, 'the first, literal, patent meaning analogically intends *a second meaning which is not given otherwise than in the first*'. This leads on to a second difference between signs and symbols, namely, the *opaqueness* of symbols: 'in distinction to technical signs, which are perfectly transparent and say only what they mean by positing the signified, symbolic signs are opaque. . . . This opaqueness is the symbol's very profundity, an inexhaustible depth.'[51]

Although Jaspers sometimes describes ciphers as metaphysical symbols, he prefers the term cipher to symbol.

> 'Cipher' . . . denotes language, the language of a reality that can be heard and addressed only thus and in no other way – while a symbol stands for something else, even though this may not exist outside the symbol. What we mean by a symbol is the other thing, which thus becomes objective and comes to be present

[51] Paul Ricoeur, 'The hermeneutics of symbols and philosophical reflection: I', in Paul Ricoeur, *The Conflict of Interpretations. Essays in Hermeneutics*, ed. Don Ihde (Evanston: Northwestern University Press, 1974), pp. 287–314; 290 (original emphasis).

in the symbol. Yet symbols may turn into elements of the cipher language.[52]

What Jaspers seems to mean here is that through the symbol that which is symbolized is made present to us. It is the objectification of that which it symbolizes. Ciphers, however, are language that is '*not* accessible through the identity of thing and symbol in the symbol itself'.[53] For Jaspers a symbol symbolizes something within and not beyond the sphere of the subject–object dichotomy.

What distinguishes ciphers from signs and symbols is that 'ciphers mean a language that is heard in ciphers alone, that does not refer to something else, and whose speaking subject is unknown, unknowable, untraceable'.[54] Ciphers do not point to objects in the world but to that which transcends the subject–object dichotomy. They are characterized by the fact that they do not map onto an object in the world and their meaning cannot be exhausted by comprehending the reality they signify: 'The significations which cannot be annulled by equating them with the object signified we call ciphers. They signify, but they do not signify a specific thing. The content is only in the cipher and does not exist outside it.'[55]

Ciphers are both subjective and objective. Jaspers writes: 'Ciphers are objective: in them something is heard that comes to meet man. Ciphers are subjective: man creates them by his way of apprehending, his way of thinking, his

[52] Jaspers, *Philosophical Faith and Revelation*, p. 95, n. 1.
[53] Jaspers, *Der philosophische Glaube angesichts der Offenbarung*, p. 157 (emphasis added); my translation.
[54] Jaspers, *Philosophical Faith and Revelation*, p. 123.
[55] Jaspers, *Philosophy is for Everyman*, p. 93. It is here that Jaspers differs from Tillich, who holds that 'the symbol participates in the reality of that for which it stands'. Paul Tillich, *Systematic Theology* (London: SCM Press, 1951), p. 239.

powers of conception.'[56] The objective dimension, then, is that ciphers do indeed point beyond themselves, namely to Transcendence. The subjective dimension is that the language in which the confrontation with Transcendence is expressed is a human creation. We use human language to express a reality which transcends human language. Ciphers are both prisms and mirrors. We see through them to Transcendence and in doing so we see ourselves and become ourselves.

Ciphers cannot function as pointers to Transcendence, however, unless they are ambiguous. Univocal ciphers would result in the confusion of an objective reality in the world with Transcendence. The ambiguity of ciphers prevents this and, furthermore, acts as an impulse in our struggle towards authentic existence. Jaspers writes:

> The great step in which man transforms himself occurs when the supposed corporeality of Transcendence is given up as deceptive and the ambiguous cipher language is heard instead – when the contents that have been conceived and visualized are stripped of objective reality. Instead of tangibles there remain ciphers open to infinitely varied interpretation.[57]

This ambiguity is possible, Jaspers argues, only when we reject the corporeality of ciphers and engage in what he terms the 'suspension of ciphers',[58] both of which entail a refusal to treat ciphers as if they were objective or embodied realities.

Their ambiguity means that ciphers are not objectively verifiable. Because they do not belong to the realm of

[56] Jaspers, *Philosophy is for Everyman*, pp. 93–4.
[57] Jaspers, *Philosophical Faith and Revelation*, p. 92.
[58] Ibid., p. 93.

knowledge, they are not accessible to 'rational', objective thinking, and 'cannot be experienced and verified as generally valid'.[59] Consequently, ciphers are not compelling. We cannot 'prove' their validity to others. Where, then, does the truth of the ciphers lie? What is the appropriate way of 'thinking' the ciphers if objective, rational thought is inappropriate? To answer these questions we must turn to Jaspers' analysis of the relation between the ciphers and Existenz.

The interpretation of ciphers: Existenz

How does the human being make sense of the ciphers? For the human being to gain a glimmer of the Transcendent Being which the ciphers mediate, the ciphers must be deciphered. Transcendence, however, is not an 'objective' reality, but transcends the subject–object dichotomy. It is thus not accessible to objective approaches. As we have seen, cognition is not the appropriate stance towards ciphers. Nor is the interpretation of ciphers concerned with establishing their 'valid' meaning, for this would entail the objectification of the ciphers through the attempt to translate them into philosophically acceptable concepts.[60] The attempt to establish the 'validity' of ciphers imposes objectifying thinking upon them and thereby drags the ciphers down into the distorting context of the subject–object dichotomy. All attempts to prove or explain the ciphers destroys them, for such attempts annihilate precisely that which allows the ciphers to come alive for human beings and open the way to Transcendence, namely, existential participation.

The means by which the deciphering of the ciphers takes

[59] Ibid., p. 92.
[60] Jaspers, *Philosophy*, III, pp. 130–1.

place, then, is not by knowledge, but by existential decision on the part of the human being in response to the message originating from Being-itself. As Jaspers puts it in *Philosophy is for Everyman* it is 'only existential experience [that] unlocks the meaning of the ciphers'.[61] And he writes in *Philosophical Faith and Revelation* that 'What speaks in ciphers is not heard by any intellect seeking sense experience and proof, only by the freedom of Existenz, with which Transcendence communicates in that language.'[62] The question of Transcendence is thus not a problem of rationality but of existential decision. The truth of ciphers is accessible only through our appropriation of them, which enables us to live in their world. This appropriation, however,

> is more than historical understanding. Appropriation means in the struggle of the ciphers to allow the ciphers to become the language of a reality, a language which touches us in so far as we are existentially open. This language is thrust aside when it is experienced as a language of unreality or that of an alien force, or as an enticement into darkness, untruthfulness, and evil.[63]

There is no such thing as a neutral, objective comprehension of the ciphers. 'The interpreter', Jaspers writes, 'does not come close to them until he lives them.'[64] The comprehension of ciphers is not so much a mode of knowledge as a mode of being.

[61] Jaspers, *Philosophy is for Everyman*, p. 96.
[62] Jaspers, *Philosophical Faith and Revelation*, p. 96.
[63] Jaspers, *Der philosophische Glaube angesichts der Offenbarung*, pp. 492–3 (my translation); *Philosophical Faith and Revelation*, p. 332.
[64] Jaspers, *Philosophical Faith and Revelation*, p. 119.

To put it another way, transcendent Being is accessible to human beings only when they respond properly to it. Ciphers can mediate Being-itself only when the human being is receptive to them. The language of ciphers is audible only to those whose existence is structured in such a way that they become responsive to Transcendence. If we are existentially deaf, then we will be unable to hear the transcendent message contained in the apparently objective language of the ciphers.[65] Such receptiveness requires personal commitment, confession to the limited nature of knowledge, and engagement in the quest for the truth. It means a transformation of one's existence. Jaspers writes:

> Reading ciphers is so unlike comprehending a being independent of me that it is quite impossible unless I am myself. Transcendent being in itself is independent of me but inaccessible as such; only things in the world have the mode of accessibility. About transcendence I learn only so much as I become myself. Its presence – constant in itself – is dimmed by my flagging; my extinction, my reduction to the existence of pure consciousness at large, makes it disappear. Seized upon, it is to me the only being there is, the being that remains what it is without me.[66]

For Jaspers, then, a cipher is a cipher only through the existential involvement of the human being. That is, the cipher is dependent for its cipher function on existential participation. The cipher makes its content, namely Transcendence, present to us only in so far as we become existentially authentic. Ciphers and existential appropriation are correlative concepts. There is a dialectical relation-

[65] Jaspers, *Philosophy*, III, p. 132.
[66] Ibid., pp. 131–2.

ship present between the cipher and the recipient of the cipher that is absent in our comprehension of symbols.

The inspiration of the Bible

With appropriate corrections and modifications, Jaspers' conception of ciphers provides us with a useful tool for articulating the nature of inspiration. The Bible is inspired because it provides the human being with ciphers of Transcendence; its inspiration rests on its ability to shed light on human existence by creating an existential openness on the part of human beings to Transcendence. To borrow a term used by Jaspers of his own philosophy, the Bible is *Existenzerhellung*, elucidation of existence.[67] That is, the Bible can be said to be inspired by virtue of its ability to offer existential elucidation to the reader by providing the reader with ciphers. These shed light on existence by pointing beyond themselves to the Transcendent or, to use the more familiar biblical and theological term, God. There are several questions that arise here. What are the ciphers in the Bible? How are they appropriated? How is God involved in the ciphers? Why should we speak of the Bible's mediation of ciphers as 'inspiration'? Our first question is to consider the nature of the biblical ciphers.

The ciphers of the Bible

The theologian should articulate and explicate the biblical ciphers with considerable reserve, for in giving an account of them they can all too easily be dragged down into objectivity, emptied of their ambiguity and thereby divested of their meaning. Although the cipher content

[67] This is the title of the second volume of his *Philosophy*.

can be philosophically extracted from the biblical texts, the ciphers' mediation of Transcendence can take place only when one goes beyond this philosophical interpretation to an existential appropriation of the ciphers.

A similar state of affairs applies to great literature, especially poetry. If poetry is reduced to prose, something essential is lost, even if the prose 'translation' expresses accurately the conceptual content of the poem. The language used and the images evoked by the poem are intrinsic and essential to the poem's impact upon the reader or listener. This parallels the function of the biblical ciphers. In extracting the cipher content from the biblical texts we are in fact distorting it.

Similarly, myths do not lack noetic content but they are not reducible to this content. Indeed, their mythological language is an important and significant medium for the articulation and mediation of this content. It is this conviction that underlies Jaspers' critique of Bultmann's programme of demythologization in their controversy of 1953–1954.[68] The imagery of myth expresses metaphorically and dialectically what cannot be stated by means of rational thought alone. Bultmann's dependence on Heidegger's *Daseinsanalyse*, Jaspers argues, blinds him to the fact that the symbolic language of myth utterly transcends the scientific approach. In a sense, the mythological language of the biblical ciphers helps to protect them from the objective gaze and acts as a spur to adopting an existential relationship to them. Demythologization, however, removes the ambiguity of the ciphers and translates them into an unequivocal philosophical language. The task is thus not one of *de*mythologizing but *re*mythologizing myth. It is not a question of translating the mythologically clothed biblical

[68] Karl Jaspers and Rudolf Bultmann, *Myth and Christianity*, trans. Norbert Guterman (New York: Noonday Press, 1958).

ciphers into a language that is accessible, meaningful and intelligible by today's standards. It is a question of *Ergriffenheit* – of allowing oneself to be seized by the ciphers and by the Transcendence they mediate. It is in this *Ergriffenheit* that the inspired status of the Bible lies.

What, then, are the ciphers in the Bible? Although virtually anything in the Bible can become a cipher if it is able to mediate an experience of Transcendence to the reader, there are certain ciphers whose impact is greater than others. For this reason it is helpful if we make a distinction between central and peripheral ciphers or between primary and secondary ciphers. Alternatively, as Farrer puts it, 'In the prophets, as in the apostles, we must distinguish between the master-images for which there are no equivalents, and the subordinate images by which the master-images are set forth or brought to bear.'[69] What, then, are these primary ciphers or master-images?

For Jaspers, 'God' is one of the most significant of all ciphers: The cipher of God points the human being beyond all ciphers to the transcendent ground that underlies them.[70] 'God' is the cipher of ciphers, and the ground of all other ciphers. Western thought, Jaspers claims, has produced three basic ciphers of the Divine, namely God as 'One', 'Personal' and 'Incarnate'.

The one God

God is, as Heidegger emphasizes, not a being, not even the highest being. To understand God as a being, even as the highest Being, is to drag God down into ontic being and treat him as an entity among entities. Jaspers makes a similar point when he emphasizes that 'the one God' is not a numerical concept. That is, the 'one God' is not the first or

[69] Farrer, *Glass of Vision*, p. 133.
[70] Jaspers, *Philosophical Faith and Revelation*, p. 138.

greatest of a series:

> As the number One, in particular, the cipher is not adequately conceived. It means a qualitative, not a quantitative, unity; in the external character of the mere number the cipher fades out. The numeral is ambiguous: it conveys the meaning of the cipher, the luminary that kindles the glow of the one Transcendence in the numerical One – and it may lead astray and then, in the name of merely numerical unity, spread ruinous fanaticism through the world.[71]

That is, if we conceive of God in quantitative terms it becomes necessary to defend God against rival conceptions of Transcendence. The result of this is that the one God becomes, in a wholly negative sense, a jealous God, a God of intolerance and exclusion. Consequently, the one God ceases to function as a cipher and becomes instead the ground and justification of self-will, fanaticism, despotism and oppression of the other. This destroys freedom and thereby undermines existential openness to Transcendence.

Correctly understood, however, the one God is unity and wholeness of Transcendence. The opposite of the oneness of God is polytheism, a concept which expresses the disintegration of wholeness into a series of disparate, apparently irreconcilable, competing powers. In existential terms this expresses itself in the disparateness and dissipation of human existence and, as Jaspers points out, in the experience that 'there are many powers battling with each other in ourselves, and through ourselves'.[72]

The one God is available to us only in so far as we draw

[71] Jaspers, *Philosophical Faith and Revelation*, p. 138.
[72] Ibid., p. 137.

together the disparate elements of the self into a coherent whole. But at the same time it is through the cipher of the one God that we receive the power to consolidate ourselves. The 'one God' acts as a regulative concept for the construction of the self.[73] It provides, to employ Macquarrie's term, a 'master possibility' for the organization of the human self. Yet simultaneously the one God remains aloof, distant and absent if we do not open ourselves to him and embark upon the process of existential self-construction:

> The One is simultaneously the Absolute of the one Transcendence and the One as the guiding force *in* me in my historical actualization. The One is thus infinitely distant, inconceivable, unrecognizable, the ground of all ontic being ['der Grund alles Seienden'], and on the other hand, very near when I am given to myself in my freedom and strike out on the way of becoming identical with myself.[74]

We ourselves become the cipher for the one God in so far as we impose unity on our existence through opening ourselves up to Transcendence, something we do only by accepting the cipher of the one God as an avenue to Transcendence.

In the Bible the cipher of the one God is expressed and qualified by means of such secondary or subordinate ciphers as divine kingship and judgement. These concretize the oneness of God and articulate the claim that God has and makes upon human beings. Such secondary ciphers express the existential seriousness of the relationship to Transcendent Being.

[73] Jaspers, *Chiffren der Transzendenz* (Munich: Piper, 1970), p. 52.
[74] Ibid.; original emphasis.

The personal God

The second great cipher in the Western tradition is the 'personal God'. The cipher of the personal God, Jaspers argues, enables the personhood of human beings. 'This personal divinity', he writes, is

> that through which the human being becomes a human being – becomes a personal human being . . . One can say that to the degree in which Transcendence assumes the cipher of the personal God, to that same degree the personal character of the human being increases. Because human beings can become personalities or persons, in their becoming such they touch this objectivity of Transcendence in the Encompassing which opens itself in the cipher of the Personal God.[75]

The concept of the person or personality of God, then, expresses the insight that it is through and in our own personhood that we come to sustain a relationship to Transcendence. Our personhood is illuminated by the cipher of the personal God, which meets us as a call to become persons. In thinking through the personhood of God we think through what it is for each of us individually to be a person.[76]

The Bible is permeated with references to the person and personality of God: God is merciful, just, loving, mild, strict, angry, jealous and so on. From the Christian perspective – one which Jaspers did not share – the cipher of the personhood of God finds its fullest expression in the Trinity. This central Christian cipher expresses not only the mystery of Transcendence, but also its living, inter-

[75] Ibid., pp. 60–1.
[76] Jaspers, *Philosophical Faith and Revelation*, pp. 152–3.

personal and interrelational nature. Above all it indicates that, from the Christian perspective, Transcendence is not so transcendent that it exists outside time and history, but interacts and engages with human persons within history.

The incarnation

The third great cipher of Transcendence in Western civilization is the incarnation. Jaspers, however, is highly critical of this doctrine on the ground of its alleged 'corporeality'. In affirming that God became present as a specific human being at a particular place and time, Jaspers claims, Christianity has reduced Divinity to a physical reality,[77] thus robbing the cipher of its ambiguity and dissolving Transcendence into immanence. Thereby the dialectic of concealment and unconcealment which is so important for the existential appropriation of the cipher of God is lost through the embodiment of Transcendence in the cipher of the incarnation.

For Jaspers, then, 'The great step in which the human being transforms himself occurs when the supposed corporeality of Transcendence is given up as deceptive and the ambiguous cipher language is heard instead.'[78] Just as no reality should be identified with a cipher, so too should no cipher be identified with Transcendence. As Jaspers puts it, 'Ciphers are never the reality of Transcendence itself, only its possible language.'[79] Consequently, it is essential that the human being must not be limited to or by one overriding cipher, but should 'float' among a multitude of polyvalent ciphers.

If the incarnation did indeed reduce Transcendence to an unambiguous physical reality in which we encounter God

[77] Ibid., pp. 145–8.
[78] Jaspers, *Philosophical Faith and Revelation*, p. 92.
[79] Ibid., p. 93.

directly and immediately, then Jaspers' rejection of Christianity on the grounds of its corporeality might be justified. Jaspers' criticism may be appropriate to a certain dogmatizing tendency in Christianity, in so far as this tendency eliminates existential ambiguity and reduces the need for existential commitment. There has been a tendency in Christian doctrine to reduce the ciphers and symbols of the Bible to quasi-objective propositions, a procedure which eliminates the ambiguity and existential tension essential for their reception and appropriation. But this need not be the case, and is certainly not the case with the doctrine of the incarnation. We are not confronted with the choice 'Jesus as cipher or Jesus Christ as embodied God',[80] as Jaspers puts it. Christ's cipher function is dependent on and anchored in his embodiment of God. Christ embodies the Transcendent and expresses in his person the existential and epistemological overcoming of the subject–object dichotomy, a fact which is expressed in the New Testament's claim that Christ is one with the Father (John 10.30). This embodiment of Transcendence does not reduce the Christ-cipher to unambiguity, however. Indeed, the incarnation functions as a cipher precisely *because* of its ambiguity. Christ's divine status was not an objective, empirical reality to his contemporaries, as the ambivalent reaction he evoked among his fellow Jews indicates. Christ's divinity, as Kierkegaard points out, was concealed beneath a human incognito. To say that God has become human is not to affirm that God has become an objective reality which can be acknowledged and appropriated without effort on the part of the human being. The God-man is not an elimination of the ambiguity and contradiction that drives the human being's quest for

[80] Jaspers, *Der philosophische Glaube angesichts der Offenbarung*, p. 227; *Philosophical Faith and Revelation*, p. 146.

Transcendence, but constitutes their most radical intensification. Through the ambiguous and paradoxical conjoining of divinity and humanity in his person, Christ does not remove the existential tension of our relationship to Transcendence, but focuses and concretizes it by confronting each human being with the question: 'Who do you say that I am?' (Mark 8.29)

The cipher of the incarnation is important in preventing the relationship to Transcendence from dissolving into vagueness, a danger that is constantly lurking at Jaspers' door. Olson comments:

> throughout his writings there is the pronounced tendency to speak about Transcendence and the Encompassing in general and very rarely in relation to what might be regarded as concrete examples of their symbolization. This is particularly disturbing in view of Jaspers' continuous insistence on the historic character of Transcendence.[81]

Jaspers' highly abstract, disembodied Transcendence lacks substantiality. This is a serious problem in a philosophy that emphasizes the existential concreteness of the relationship to Transcendence. Olson again:

> It is simply impossible . . . to 'purify transcendence,' as Jaspers puts it, of all its presumably histrionic *accoutrements* and still have Transcendence that is convincing . . . apart from a careful analysis of the rich textures of the mythic-symbolic in its historic givenness, the specificity of Transcendence is nullified through reification in the conceptual abstractions of cognitive transcending.[82]

[81] Olson, *Transcendence and Hermeneutics*, p. 114.
[82] Ibid., p. 115.

The appropriation of ciphers

Although the biblical ciphers point to Transcendence, they do so only when we refrain from treating them objectively. To treat the Bible objectively is to reduce it to existential flatness. The Bible itself opposes such treatment. It is permeated with contradictions and inconsistencies. But in this respect it is, as Jaspers points out, like life, and dealing with the Bible is like dealing with life itself.[83] But these contradictions and inconsistencies do not detract from the value and significance of the Bible. On the contrary, they constitute an essential aspect of its capacity to point to Transcendence. Far from undermining the Bible, they are an essential feature of its inspired status. For the contradictions create existential ambiguity, an ambiguity that can be resolved only through the existential concern of the individual in his or her interaction with Transcendence. As Jaspers puts it, 'one must move in the contradictions in order to participate in the truth which becomes brighter only through these contradictions'.[84] Throughout its history the Church has frequently succumbed to the tendency to harmonize the tensions in the Bible, but this removes the necessity of struggling with the ciphers. As we saw earlier, it is precisely this struggle that opens up the possibility of a relation to Transcendence.

To treat the biblical ciphers objectively is to impose the subject–object dichotomy upon the transcendent reality to which they point and thereby reduce them to objects. This causes the biblical ciphers to cease to function as ciphers, because in treating them as objective statements we stand over against them in a subject–object relationship, which thwarts the ciphers' ability to point beyond the subject–

[83] Jaspers, *Philosophical Faith and Revelation*, p. 333.
[84] Jaspers, *Der philosophische Glaube angesichts der Offenbarung*, p. 495; *Philosophical Faith and Revelation*, p. 333.

object dichotomy to Transcendence. It is thus mistaken to treat the biblical material as a description of objective facts or, to use Melanchthon's description of the Bible, as a compendium of Christian doctrine.

Our relation to the biblical texts should therefore be not objective but participatory. The meaning of the Bible is not conveyed by merely objective presentation of its content. The interpretation of the Bible is not a case of reconstructing the events or thought-world that gave rise to the biblical texts, but of existential communication with the writers of these texts and their engagement with Transcendence; it is a personal engagement with their struggle with the question of God. The biblical texts remain closed to us unless they are interpreted existentially as something *pro me*. It is necessary for the reader to go beyond an objective–historical attitude to the texts to a consciousness of the existential demand that these texts make upon the reader. This point is well made by Kierkegaard in his theory of indirect communication.[85] The truths of human existence, i.e., existential and religious truths, truths concerning what it means to be truly human, cannot be communicated directly and objectively in the way that it is possible to teach someone woodwork or mathematics. In order truly to 'learn' such truths we must appropriate them and make them our own.

This existential reading of the Bible does not reduce it to subjectivity, however, but frees its meaning for the experience of the reader. The biblical texts become

[85] Kierkegaard, *Concluding Unscientific Postscript to Philosophical Fragments*, ed. and trans. Howard V. Hong and Edna H. Hong, 2 vols, (Princeton, NJ: Princeton University Press, 1992), I, pp. 72–80, 242–50; *Søren Kierkegaard's Journals and Papers*,' ed. and trans. Howard V. Hong and Edna H. Hong (Bloomington, IN: Indiana University Press, 1967–78), 7 vols, I, pp. 648–57. See also my *Kierkegaard as Negative Theologian* (Oxford: Clarendon Press, 1993), 58–69.

essential to the individual as the hermeneutical framework within which the individual comprehends his or her existence and without which the self-being of that individual is diminished. It is impossible to grasp Transcendence fully, but in the reader's dynamic interaction with the Bible there remains a trace of Transcendence, a trace acquired not directly but indirectly through existential appropriation.

The biblical writers are those who have (temporarily) overcome the subject–object dichotomy and have gained an insight into Transcendent Being. They have existentially but not ontologically transcended the subject–object dichotomy, for ontologically we always remain situated in this dichotomy. This existential transcendence and the insight it brings are necessarily expressed in language conditioned by the subject–object dichotomy and therefore cannot be mediated *directly* to us. The biblical texts become meaningful only when we ourselves transcend the subject–object dichotomy. At the same time, however, it is the biblical texts that can assist us to overcome the subject–object dichotomy. This means that the readers are called upon to sustain a dialectical relationship with these texts. They have to bring an openness to the texts if these are to speak to them and yet at the same time these texts can open up deeper levels of existence to the individual and provide an insight into Being. To approach the Bible without the correct existential attitude will result in a misunderstanding of it, for the biblical ciphers that mediate Transcendence will then mistakenly be taken to have an *objective* reference. This means that the individual is still rooted in the subject–object dichotomy and therefore unable to intuit the significance of the biblical ciphers.

Penetration into Transcendence by means of the ciphers is not a one-off event, which once it has taken place is over and done with. It is a continual encounter, an encounter that must be lived out in each individual's life. It is an ongoing formation and transformation of the individual's existence.

The biblical ciphers, then, cannot be 'proved' objectively, but are intelligible and meaningful only when the individual human being receives them with the correct existential response. In Christian language this is understood in terms of the operation of the Spirit who, as Paul puts it, 'searches everything, even the depths of God' and enables our carnal minds to perceive spiritual truth (1 Cor 2.10–15; Rom 8.15–16). Our existential response to the ciphers is the inner testimony of the Spirit, which assists us in our assent and obedience to scripture.

Summary

In summary, the inspiration of the Bible is situated in three areas. Inspiration is a feature of human being. In the language adopted in this study, inspiration is the opening up of human being to Transcendence and the (trans)formation of human existence in the light of Transcendence. It is in their capacity to encourage self-transformation on the part of the reader that the inspired status of the biblical texts resides. But this 'existential inspiration' and grounding of human being in Transcendence is not self-produced. It comes about through engagement with the ciphers of Transcendence communicated by the Bible. In so far as the existential coherence of the human being is dependent on the ciphers, the source of these ciphers, namely the Bible, can be said to be inspired. Finally, inspiration is situated in Transcendence-itself. In his or her engagement with the biblical texts and subsequent existential development, the human being ascribes the existential coherence acquired through such engagement not to his or her own powers, but to the power of Transcendent Being.

These three factors and the dialectical relationship that exists between them constitute the complex phenomenon that is inspiration. To emphasize one at the expense of the others results in a distortion of biblical inspiration and its reduction either to a purely human phenomenon or to something that is unbelievable in the light of the biblical phenomena.

God's relation to the Bible

Thus far we have considered the question of inspiration from the perspective of human existence. The Bible is inspired, we have argued, because it has the power to shed light on human existence and point us towards Transcendence. Does this mean that there is no objective dimension to the content of the Bible? Does it mean that everything can be swallowed up in subjective categories, that the Bible is merely a description of the contents of religious consciousness? To claim this would again be to ignore the subject–object dichotomy by this time reducing everything to subjectivity. It must be stressed, however, that the individual who responds to the ciphers does not thereby 'create' God. Although we might speak loosely and say that, for the respondent, God becomes 'alive' for the first time as a result of the existential impact of the ciphers, God must already be present in order for the ciphers to possess the capacity to impact upon the human being. This is well expressed by Farrer, who comments that 'The problem of our knowing God . . . is never a problem of his being made present, but always of our being able to apprehend his presence'.[86]

Now it is true that we can never fully penetrate into

[86] Farrer, *The Glass of Vision*, p. 86.

Transcendence and therefore can never arrive at the position where we can view Transcendence/Being/God from an objective standpoint. Nevertheless, the Bible does contain an objective dimension but, paradoxically, it is an objectivity that is accessible only through subjectivity. The knowledge the Bible provides is not 'objective' in the normal sense, for the knowledge which it provides is first and foremost existential knowledge. That is, it sheds light on the nature of human existence and how human life is best lived. The Bible, as we said earlier, is concerned not with information but with being. This does not mean, however, that the epistemological content of the Bible has no objective dimension or cannot be objectively expressed. Many aspects of the existential knowledge contained in the Bible can indeed be given objective expression. Indeed, it is this objective expression that gives rise to doctrines and creeds. However, the crucial thing is that this objectivity is not central, but secondary to, and dependent on, the existential impact and content of these statements. We can break down the objectivity of the Bible into the following forms.

The ontological priority of God

Human subjectivity contains a dynamic that leads it to ascribe objectivity to God. There are two reasons for this. First, the subjective development of the human being is dependent upon his or her belief that it has an objective reference in God. The existential development the human being undergoes in appropriating and responding to ciphers is sustainable only when that individual believes that he or she is relating to a reality that exists independently of the human mind. In other words, the subjective impact of biblical ciphers is not possible without positing an objective, divine source. Ciphers lose their subjective impact for the believer if they are regarded as purely subjective with no reference to a God who exists independently of those ciphers. Secondly, and closely connected with the previous point, although the individual arrives at a belief in Transcendence as a result of subjective, existential development, he or she is compelled by this development to posit the ontological priority of the concept of God. Belief in Transcendence might be said to be a posteriori in the sense that it is something that is arrived at as the result of the individual's personal subjective and existential development, but it is a priori in the sense that the believer comes to realize that this existential development is possible only if God is prior to this development. In the Bible itself, this insight can be found in Jeremiah's conviction that he was called by God before his conception (Jer 1.5) and in such statements as 'We loved because he loved us first' (1 John 4.19). In theological terms, this is the experience of *grace*.

This insight opens the door to a series of secondary theological concepts. Thus one way in which believers may come to speak of their conviction that their subjective, existential development is possible only on positing the ontological priority of God is by talking in terms of God taking the initiative. Once one has accepted the reality of God, one is forced to the conclusion that God exists prior to and independently of the subjective means by which one has arrived at this conclusion. It is thus appropriate to speak, as does Farrer, of a 'double personal agency' of the biblical texts.[87] The Bible is written by human beings, but God is also active in these texts in so far as they become prisms through which he can be glimpsed. But we cannot view this agency from the divine perspective. Our acceptance of divine involvement in these texts is a leap of faith,

[87] Farrer, *The Glass of Vision*, p. 33.

but not a blind one. It is because of the ability of these texts to resonate in our being that we attribute them to divine initiative. God is not directly involved in the production of the biblical texts, however, but God is the reality to which the authors of the text respond. The texts are the result of the author's relation to Transcendence. There is no special commission to write. Writing is merely one of several possible responses to Transcendence.

The existential 'objectivity' of biblical truth

The believer makes the Bible's existential insights and religious truths 'objective' in his or her own existence. The human being is called upon not merely to give intellectual assent to the truth but to embody it in his or her own life. When the human being becomes the truth by living according to the transcendental insights provided by the ciphers, then the truth acquires an objective existence in the being of that person and, through his or her actions, acquires an objective, 'empirical' existence in the world. As Barth puts it, 'To say "Lord, Lord" is not enough. What matters is to do the will of God if we are to know His grace and truth – for that is the inspiration of the Bible.'[88] It is here that the significance of the ethical 'commandments' of the Bible and the existence of the Church lies. The Church is the community in which the ciphers are made objective realities. The authority of the Bible becomes an objective reality in the life of the Church and in the Church's life in the world. This is the only way the 'validity' of the Bible can be established. The Bible is a collection of ciphers that express religious existence. These ciphers, and consequently the validity of the Bible itself, can be tested only by living the kind of existence to which they point.

[88] Karl Barth, *Church Dogmatics*, I/2 (Edinburgh: T&T Clark, 1956), pp. 533–4.

Conclusions and implications

In our opening chapter we spoke of the mystery of inspiration and quoted Farrer's comment when referring to St Paul and St John, that 'the moving of these men's minds, or of any men's minds, by divine direction is in any case a profound and invisible mystery, as is the whole relation of the creature to the creator'.[89] At the end of our discussion, the mysterious nature of inspiration has not been dispelled, nor should it be. It is not the task of the writer on inspiration to remove the mystery, but to let it stand in all its clarity. Above all, it is the task of the writer on inspiration to make clear the existential significance of inspiration and the life-transforming nature of the biblical texts.

We do not have direct unmediated access to the depth that is Transcendent Being; nor do we have access to the deep and powerful currents that motivated the inspired biblical writers. The mechanisms and processes by which the Divine Mind engaged with the human mind of the inspired biblical writers remain hidden from us. We do have access, however, to the surface manifestations of this engagement, namely the biblical ciphers in which the divine inspiration of the biblical writers came to expression. But these ciphers come alive for us only when we see through them to the depth from which they have emerged. It is precisely this 'seeing through' that constitutes inspiration for us, for it is only when we allow the ciphers to address and inspire us that we too can see through them to the divine ground that underlies them. This requires, as we saw earlier, a creative movement on the part of the readers in which they appropriate the biblical ciphers and make them their own.

[89] Farrer, *The Glass of Vision*, p. 113.

The authority of the Bible rests in its ability to provide an avenue into Transcendence and shed light on the deeper meaning of human existence. In so far as the Bible or, more accurately, the ciphers in the Bible are able to achieve this, it can be said to be inspired. The Bible's universal authority lies in its potential to point all human beings to Transcendence. Having said this, we must never forget that the Bible is not an objective description of Transcendence. To understand the Bible in this way would be to impose the subject–object dichotomy upon it and thereby empty its ciphers of their existential significance. The Bible is only ever an expression of what God is for us. It is not an expression of what God is in himself but an expression of the reality of God in relation to human beings. It is this human pole in the relationship that explains the problematic material in the Bible, which is accounted for by the human struggle to articulate the experience of Transcendence.

Situating inspiration in the reader's response to the biblical ciphers makes it possible to accommodate some of the problems we encountered with word-centred and non-verbal theories of inspiration. It removes the problem of the apparent end of inspiration in the apostolic age by closing the gap between the inspiration of the biblical writers and the inspiration of the reader. There is no essential difference between the inspiration of the biblical writers and later readers of the Bible. The source is one and the same, namely, the relation to Transcendence. Both are inspired in so far as their being is opened up to Transcendence through interaction with Transcendence. This is expressed theologically in the assertion that the Holy Spirit is responsible for inspiring both the biblical writer and the reader of the Bible. The difference between them lies in the fact that the biblical writers' recording of their experience of Transcendence acts as the framework for future mediation and experience of Transcendence.

By situating inspiration in the reader's response to the biblical ciphers, we – in contrast to non-verbal theories of inspiration – retain a significant role not merely for the underlying message of the Bible but for the text itself. The tension the text creates through its ambiguity and self-contradictory nature is a constituent element of the inspired and inspiring nature of the Bible, but only in so far as the reader engages with these texts in existential concern and allows this tension to point him or her through and beyond the text to Transcendence.

I would like to conclude this study by briefly mapping out some of the implications of this understanding of inspiration.

The problematic material in the Bible

The reader-centred conception of inspiration advanced in this study is able to accommodate the problematic material in the Bible by assigning to such material an important role in opening up human being to Transcendence. Problematic material in the Bible heightens the ambiguity of the texts, and ambiguity, as we saw earlier, is essential for the reader's existential commitment to the biblical ciphers. If we treat the Bible with existential seriousness, then the problematic material presents no obstacle; on the contrary, its problematic material acts as a spur to existential seriousness. The crucial point is not the empirical validity or accuracy of what is said but following the pointer to Transcendence that the text provides.

It is this insight that lies behind the use of allegory in the ancient Church. The importance of allegorical interpretation is its recognition of the tensions and ambiguities of the biblical text and the importance of the problematic material in the Bible for a relationship with God. Origen recognized that this material points the reader beyond the surface meaning of the text to a deeper spiritual meaning.[90] The weakness of the allegorical method, however, is its attempt to remove these tensions at the level of conceptuality rather than existential commitment, and the arbitrariness of the manner in which it carried this out. The approach adopted in this study advocates keeping open the ambiguity and tension created by the problematic material, precisely because this heightens the Bible's existential impact. However, this material can play a positive role only when it is anchored to the central ciphers. The Church is important for the discernment of the central ciphers because it provides an educative context (albeit a human and flawed one) within which the impact of the ciphers can be most profoundly experienced.

Our reader-centred conception of inspiration allows us to ascribe inspired status to texts which no longer speak to us, such as the Old Testament food laws. These texts are witnesses to the human response to Transcendence and we can appreciate them as such even when we believe that for us now there are more appropriate ways of responding to Transcendence. Although much in these texts may now be alien to us and indeed have been abrogated by other strands in the biblical witness to Transcendence,[91] we can still recognize that they express the existential commitment to and appropriation of Transcendence that are essential features of the relationship. The same argument applies to the historical works of the Bible such as Joshua, Judges, Samuel, Kings and Chronicles in the Old Testament and the Acts of the Apostles in the New Testament.

[90] Origen, *On First Principles*, IV, ch. 1.

[91] The Old Testament food laws are, from the Christian perspective, abrogated by the New Testament pronouncement that all foods are clean. That is, the New Testament points the reader towards other, non-dietary ways of responding to Transcendence (Acts 10.9–16).

Such works record the response of human beings to Transcendence, and in this response we may find ciphers that can help evoke our own response to it.

In short, by situating inspiration in the reader's relation to the text, we avoid the problem of considering to what degree a particular biblical writer was inspired. For example, Luke does not seem to have been conscious of being inspired or of writing an inspired work. He seems rather to have struggled to bring various sources into a coherent unity (Luke 1.1–4). Luke may thus be a creative compiler, but it seems strange to regard such primarily editorial work as *inspired*. If we centre our understanding of inspiration on the reader's relation to the text, however, then this problem falls away. In so far as Luke's writings provide or contribute to the ciphers that open up an avenue to Transcendent Being, both the Gospel of Luke and the Acts of the Apostles can be said to be inspired.

But what of the material in the Bible that is not merely problematic but oppressive? In what sense can we speak of a work as 'inspired' that has been used as the justification for anti-Semitism, racism, sexism and homophobia? Do such uses or, rather, abuses of the Bible not undermine the claim that it is an inspired text? There are a number of replies that could be made to this objection. First, there are texts in the Bible that indicate a consciousness on the part of the biblical writers of the possible misuse and misapplication of scripture. This is at its clearest in the temptation narratives (Matt 4.1–11; Luke 4.1–13), where the devil appeals to Ps 91.11–12 in his attempt to win Jesus over. As Goldingay points out, the devil's appeal to scripture 'illustrat[es] how mere formal acknowledgement of that authority [of scripture] does not necessarily indicate any substantial acknowledgement of it'.[92] 'The appeal to

[92] Goldingay, *Models of Scripture*, p. 90.

scripture', Goldingay comments, 'can be self-serving and demonic.'[93] Against the devil's citation of Psalm 91, Jesus quotes another passage from scripture, namely, Deut 6.16, 'You shall not tempt the Lord your God' (Matt 4.7; Luke 4.12). This indicates, Goldingay points out, that 'One guideline for discerning the difference between the use and abuse of scripture . . . is to test possible applications of scripture by direct assertions of scripture elsewhere.'[94]

A second argument to support our view that the use of the Bible as a tool of oppression does not undermine its inspired status is that such uses of the Bible are based upon a misunderstanding of the nature of biblical authority. As we saw in chapter 1, biblical authority should not be understood in authoritarian terms but as exemplary and epistemic in nature. The use of the Bible as a tool of oppression is the result of applying an inadequate conception of authority to it.

Thirdly and most importantly, the misuse of the Bible as a tool of oppression is possible only when the central cipher that is Christ is displaced or assimilated to human self-interest. The Bible, being a human book in the sense that responsibility for its literary composition lies with human individuals and communities, will inevitably bear the marks of human fallenness. We should repent of the use of the Bible as an instrument of oppression, but the fact that the Bible has been misused in this way is not of itself proof of the inherently oppressive nature of the Bible. It becomes so only if we adopt a fragmentary approach to the Bible and refuse to allow it to interpret itself through, and in the light of, the Christ-cipher. The use of the Bible as a tool of oppression is a betrayal of its central cipher and a violation of the divine reality to which even the most

93 Ibid., p. 91.
94 Ibid.

problematic texts in the Bible point. The Bible itself, however, contains its own corrective against such abuse, namely, the Christ-cipher and the commandment of love that this cipher embodies. Uses of the Bible that justify oppression are contradicted and corrected by the cipher of Christ. They cannot be taken in isolation or ripped free of their moorings in the reality of Christ. The Bible in this sense is thus, as Luther puts it, *sui ipsius interpres.*[95] It contains its own principle for its interpretation, namely the Christ-cipher. The Christ-cipher is the criterion of what is true and false in the Bible.

Plenary inspiration and the gradation of scripture

The ability of our reader-centred conception of inspiration to accommodate problematic biblical phenomena allows us to continue to speak of the Bible as a whole as the Word of God, since even problematic material, first, constitutes a witness to the impact of Transcendence on the lives of human beings and, secondly, contributes to the existential tension necessary for the appropriation of the biblical ciphers. The Bible is an expression of Transcendence and describes human encounter and interaction with it. In so far as the biblical witness of this encounter stimulates our own relationship to Transcendence, the Bible as a whole can be said to be inspired.

This does not mean, however, that the whole of the Bible is inspired in the same way. There is a hierarchy or gradation of inspiration in the Bible. The inspired status of a biblical text is dependent upon its distance from the central and supreme cipher of the incarnation, which, from

[95] *D. Martin Luthers Werke*, 64 vols (Weimar: Hermann Böhlau and successor, 1883–1990), vol. 7, p. 97, line 23; cf., vol. 10/3, p. 238, line 10.

the Christian perspective, takes up and focuses the Transcendence-mediating function of the other biblical ciphers. The whole of the Bible is inspired, because as a whole it communicates Transcendence-mediating ciphers, but this does not exclude the possibility that certain texts within the Bible are more effective than others.

Criteria of inspiration and the problem of divergent interpretations

Are all responses to biblical texts equally valid? What are we to make of different and perhaps mutually inconsistent readings of the Bible? By what criteria can we decide between different responses to the ciphers? Furthermore, how do we know that the biblical writers were not deluded or simply lying when they wrote their allegedly cipher-mediating texts?

We cannot provide empirical, objective proof that will satisfy the sceptic that the biblical writers were not mistaken or motivated by a malicious intention to mislead. The significance that the Bible has imparted to the lives of generations of Christians, however, argues against it. If the Bible is a lie, then it is an existentially powerful one.

Nor is it possible to provide empirical, objective proof to support the claim that the Bible is inspired through its mediation of ciphers of Transcendence. As we saw earlier, the ciphers speak only when we become existentially attentive to them. Without such attentiveness on our part, we shall fail to be grasped by them and, locked into empirical, objectivist modes of thought, will be unconvinced by the arguments advanced in this study for the inspired status of the Bible.

There are, however, checks and balances that limit the possibility of completely arbitrary responses to the biblical ciphers. As we mentioned earlier in our discussion of the problematic material in the Bible, the central cipher from the Christian perspective is Christ. All responses to and interpretations of the biblical ciphers must be subordinated to this cipher and the commandment of love which it embodies. Readings of the biblical ciphers that result in modes of existence incompatible with the commandment of love can therefore be rejected as inappropriate responses to the biblical ciphers.

A second check on inappropriate readings of the ciphers is the Church. By 'Church' here we understand those Churches which stand in the mainstream of Christian tradition by virtue of their affirmation of the Niceno-Constantinopolitan Creed. These Churches provide what Christoph Schwöbel has aptly described as an *Interpretationsgemeinschaft* (community of interpretation).[96] That is, the collective experience of the (universal) Church provides the interpretative framework and community within which the reading of, and response to, the ciphers takes place. The Church both directs individuals to the Bible as a mediator of Transcendence and also functions as a check and balance on the cipher relationship of the individual. The Church is responsible for overseeing that the impact of the biblical ciphers on the individual produces a life of faith and worship that is in continuity with the faith and worship of previous generations of cipher-handlers. Of course, the Church is made up of fallen human beings and thus does not always function adequately as a check and balance and may indeed distort the ciphers. It too, however, stands not above but under the Word and is thus the servant and pupil of the Transcendence-mediating ciphers of the Bible. Above all, the Christ-cipher acts as a check on the activity of the

[96] Christoph Schwöbel, 'Kirche als Communio', in Wilfried Härle and Reiner Preul, *Marburger Jahrbuch Theologie, VIII: Kirche* (Marburg: N. G. Elwert, 1996), pp. 11–46; 43.

Church. There thus exists a complex dialectic between inspired text and Church in which the Church provides the framework within which interpretation of the ciphers can take place, while at the same time the Church is itself challenged by the ciphers.

A third check on inappropriate readings of the Bible lies in the subjectivity of each individual addressed by the ciphers. The degree to which the ciphers bring about existential integration is a mark of the adequacy or inadequacy of the individual's appropriation and interpretation of the ciphers. This is a check that is available first and foremost to the individual. Others cannot test to what degree another human being has become an integrated self, although there are some important pointers such as the biblical principle that 'By their fruits you shall know them' (Matt 7.16).

Biblical and non-biblical inspiration

A possible objection to the theory of inspiration developed in this study is that it may appear to be applicable to any literature – from the most trivial and banal novels through great works of literature to the religious writings of other faiths. If what is decisive is how the human being reacts to such texts and what existential gain the individual receives from a text, then it might be objected that virtually anything can count as inspired if the reader finds it edifying. This raises the question of the demarcation of biblical inspiration from the inspiration of, first, great literature; secondly, non-biblical Christian classics; and thirdly, the holy scriptures of non-Christian belief-systems.

There is clearly some overlap between biblical and literary inspiration. Thus a feature common to both types of inspiration is their attribution of atemporality to 'inspired' texts. As Roger Nash comments with regard to poetry, 'We say that poems are inspired, not just that they once were. We say that what is inspired is the poem itself, not just the poet.'[97] A similar atemporality is clearly evident in the custom of the author of the Epistle to the Hebrews of introducing citations of Old Testament passages in the *present* tense.[98] It is also expressed in Paul's comment that, 'whatever was written in former days was written *for our instruction*, that by steadfastness and by the encouragement of the scriptures we might have hope' (Rom 15.4; emphasis added). This means that the Old Testament is not a document of the past but one that speaks to us here and now. Inspired texts, whether poetical or biblical, are atemporal in the sense that their significance is not limited to the age in which they were written but transcends the historical and cultural contexts in which they were composed.

A further similarity is that in both biblical and literary inspiration the term 'inspiration' constitutes a value-judgement. To claim that a piece of writing is inspired constitutes an affirmation that it is of intrinsically higher worth or significance than other (allegedly non-inspired) writings. Ince aptly describes this type of inspiration as 'attributed inspiration', which he defines as a 'value-judgement by the reader who uses the word to describe that state which the poet must, he thinks, have experienced to write such good poetry'.[99]

Despite a certain degree of overlap between certain features of biblical and poetic inspiration, however, important differences remain. One such significant difference

[97] Roger Nash, 'The demonology of verse', *Philosophical Investigations*, 10 (1987), 299–316; 303; quoted in Clark, *Theory of Inspiration*, p. 3.

[98] See, e.g., Heb 3.7; 12.5.

[99] W. R. Ince, *The Poetic Theory of Paul Valéry: Inspiration and Technique* (Leicester: Leicester University Press, 1961), p. 8.

arises from our conception of human existence. If, as we argued earlier, the human being comprises a series of dipolar opposites which it is the task of each individual to bring into a coherent unified whole, then only literature which enables or contributes to this task can count as inspired. Consequently, literature which fails to contribute or perhaps even impedes this quest for existential coherence and stability by, for example, propagating a fragmentary or one-sided conception of the human self (e.g., hedonism), cannot on our definition be regarded as inspired.

Another response that could be made to the objection that our theory of inspiration accommodates not just the Bible but virtually all literature is based on the fact that not all texts are concerned with the human being's relationship to Transcendent Being. Literature that aims merely at entertaining the reader rather than opening up an avenue to Transcendence can thus be excluded from the class of inspired literature. The situation with great 'classic' literature is more complex.[100] The power of Shakespeare, Goethe and Dostoevsky lies not only in their pre-eminent command of their respective languages but also in their capacity to evoke and shed light on the human condition. A

[100] Wand argues that conceptions of literary inspiration are parasitical on the conception of the Bible as inspired. The term 'inspiration', Wand claims, is 'used in a secondary sense only' and 'is a journalistic and not a scientific use of the term'. To state of a secular work that it is inspired 'is to say that it is . . . worthy of comparison with the sacred Scriptures . . . In other words, the inspiration of the Bible is the substance of which the inspiration of Virgil, Shakespeare, and Goethe is the shadow.' J. W. C. Wand, *The Authority of the Scriptures* (London: A. R. Mowbray, 1949), p. 53. Even if Wand is right, however, this argument is not sufficient to indicate the presence of a qualitative difference between biblical and poetic inspiration. We must attempt to isolate as precisely as possible that element which distinguishes biblical from literary inspiration.

further feature of great literature is its capacity to capture the human condition in vivid poetic language that transcends the conceptual content of that of which is being spoken. Farrer is helpful here; speaking of the 'high inspiration of great poetry', he writes:

> The mind apprehends life in talking about it, and for the most part we talk about it piecemeal and with some exactitude, and that is the most useful way of apprehending our life for practical purposes. But in talking the language of Hamlet we may grasp our existence or the possibilities of our existence over a wide area and in a richer and more confused way. If we ask just *what* we are grasping, we are returning to the prosaic form of thought and the poetry vanishes.[101]

The need to spring the confines of prosaic, 'objective' language in order to articulate the depths of human existence is what links great literature with the Bible. There are, however, some essential differences.

In the case of literature, style, if not everything, is certainly a great deal. Literary style, however, is not decisive in the case of the Bible. Indeed, the Bible's violation of the classic rules of literary style has frequently created a problem for the Church. Distaste at the allegedly primitive style of the Bible was an issue frequently raised by opponents of Christianity in the early Church. More recently, O'Collins has pointed out that 'the charism of inspiration did not mean that *the literary level* reached by sacred writers was necessarily higher than that of other writers,' as passages such as the genealogies of 1 Chronicles 1–9 indicate. 'Inspiration', O'Collins comments, 'could

[101] Farrer, *The Glass of Vision*, p. 121.

co-exist with real dullness.'[102] Calvin, too, was conscious of the Bible's infelicitous style, but gets round the problem by arguing that

> when an unpolished simplicity, almost bordering on rudeness, makes a deeper impression than the loftiest flights of oratory, what does it indicate if not that the Holy Scriptures are too mighty in the power of truth to need the rhetorician's art?[103]

In the case of the Bible it is not so much the poetry of its language that is significant as the great images or ciphers it mediates: the one God, the personal God, the incarnation, the kingdom of God, and the sacrificial and atoning death of Christ. It is above all in the mediation of such ciphers that biblical inspiration resides. We can put this point another way by following Farrer and arguing that

> What the prophet shares with the latter-day poet . . . is the technique of inspiration chiefly: both move an incantation of images under a control. The controls are not the same, and therefore the whole nature and purpose of the two utterances go widely apart: the poet is a maker, the prophet is a mouthpiece.[104]

That is, although the prophet, like the poet, is involved in the creation of images or, in our terminology, ciphers, in the case of the prophet these ciphers are directed by the impact of Transcendent Being upon his or her existence. This impact and the subsequent consciousness of being in a relationship with Transcendence prompts the inspired

[102] O'Collins, *Fundamental Theology*, p. 232.
[103] Calvin, *Institutes* I. viii. 1.
[104] Farrer, *The Glass of Vision*, p. 129.

individual to conceive of the ciphers he creates as the result not of poetic genius but of the guidance of Transcendent Being.

A further point is that it is questionable whether great literature can be said to throw light on the human being's relation to Transcendence. In their explorations of the tragic dimension of human being, writers such as Shakespeare, Goethe and Dostoevsky expose and articulate our human need for Transcendent Being, but they do not themselves answer or fulfil this need. It is not just reflection on the human condition that motivates the biblical writer but above all the impact of the Transcendent. Our conception of inspiration as the textual mediation and existential appropriation of Transcendent Being would thus exclude such works as inspired. The profundity and beauty of the works of great writers like Shakespeare may prompt us to speak of them as 'inspired', but this is a purely secular use of the term, for the relationship of human being to Transcendent Being is not the central concern of such authors.[105] Although the Bible, like other great classic literature, articulates the human condition in language that is often (though not always) of great power and beauty, it contains a third level or dimension which is absent from secular inspired writings, namely the creation or opening up of an avenue to Transcendent Being.

But what of the non-biblical Christian classic? There are works of post-biblical Christian literature that may have the power to move us more than certain parts of the Bible. This is a point made by O'Collins, who argues that 'we

[105] Farrer suggests that the question of the relationship between the inspiration of the Bible and that of great literature is perhaps the wrong question and should be reversed: 'Should we ask what is the relation between religious inspiration and great poetry, or should we not rather ask how the inspiration of great poetry ever came to be secularized?' (Farrer, *The Glass of Vision*, 117).

should . . . pull back from claiming that inspiration necessarily entailed a high *religious quality and effect* which lifted the books of the Bible above all non-inspired writings for all time'. Experience proves, he argues, 'how Augustine's *Confessions*, the *Imitation of Christ* and the works of Teresa of Avila enjoy a much deeper religious impact than the Letter of Jude, 2 Maccabees and all those sexual regulations from Leviticus'.[106] This, however, is an unhelpful way of putting the problem and sets up a false dichotomy. The less central parts of the Bible are part of the primary response of human being to Transcendent Being. Non-biblical spiritual works are a secondary response arising from the impact of biblical ciphers on the non-biblical writer. They are thus dependent upon and formulated within the framework provided by the Bible, of which even the most mundane and apparently uninspired passages form a part.[107]

The situation with regard to the holy scriptures of other, non-Christian belief-systems is more complex. Here we are confronted with works that seem to fulfil the two criteria of secular inspiration, namely, exploration of the human condition and beauty of expression, and also the criterion of religious inspiration, namely, articulation of the relationship between human being and Transcendent Being. There is in my opinion no reason why we should not accept the possibility that the holy scriptures of other belief-systems may function as avenues to Transcendence. Our interpretation of the inspiration of the Bible in terms of the existential response to the biblical ciphers should not be

[106] O'Collins, *Fundamental Theology*, p. 232; original emphasis.

[107] Cf., Schleiermacher's comment that 'all explanatory and systematizing works, which as presentations of Christian piety have less originality and independence, are only aids to the understanding of the original testimonies or compilations drawn from them' (*Christian Faith*, § 129, pp. 594–5).

understood to mean that the Bible must be the *only* source of existential truth for the human being. This would be to commit the mistake of objectifying the existential content of the Bible and confusing it with that to which it points. Being, Transcendence and God are realities that cannot be encompassed by any human writings, no matter how sublime. The emphasis on the Bible as a collection of ciphers of existential truth does not mean that there are no other possible ciphers that may be capable of conveying existential truth and pointing to Transcendence. Indeed, Christianity can learn from a creative engagement with the ciphers provided by other faiths. When we speak of the inspiration of the Bible, this should not be understood as an authoritarian claim, which, as we saw in our discussion in chapter one, is an inappropriate conception of biblical authority. To claim that the Bible is inspired is not to demean other writings but is rather an invitation to engage with the biblical texts. It is an invitation and a promise that those who engage with these ancient writings will have levels of being opened up to them that would otherwise remain obscure or opaque. This does not preclude us from recognizing the possibility of other mediators of Transcendence and other ciphers in the religious writings of other faiths. Despite this openness to non-Christian ciphers, however, the Christian position will be to insist on the centrality and supremacy of the primary cipher, namely Christ, and subordinate all other ciphers to it.

In conclusion, the Bible is a witness to the impact of Transcendence on the lives of existentially concerned human beings, a witness that can serve as a source of and inspiration for our own affirmation of and commitment to Transcendence. The more we put ourselves to school under scripture, as Gore puts it, and employ it for our spiritual education, the more the inspired status of scripture will become apparent. The last word, however, goes to Jaspers, who, despite his reservations about Christianity, recognized the profundity of the biblical ciphers: 'The Bible is as rich as life. It does not document one faith; it is an arena in which possibilities of faith vie with each other for the depth of the divine.'[108]

[108] Jaspers, *Philosophical Faith and Revelation*, p. 333.

Bibliography

Abbott, Walter M. (ed.), *The Documents of Vatican II* (London: Geoffrey Chapman, 1967).

Abraham, William, *The Divine Inspiration of Holy Scripture* (Oxford: Oxford University Press, 1981).

Achtemeier, Paul J., *The Inspiration of Scripture* (Philadelphia: Westminster Press, 1980).

Alexander, Archibald, *Evidences of the Authenticity, Inspiration, and Canonical Authority of the Holy Scriptures* (Philadelphia: Presbyterian Board of Publications, 1836).

Alonso Schökel, Luis, *The Inspired Word: Scripture in the Light of Language and Literature*, trans. Francis Martin (London: Burns & Oates, 1967).

Archer, Gleason L., 'The witness of the Bible to its own inerrancy', in James Montgomery Boice (ed.), *The Foundation of Biblical Authority*, (Grand Rapids: Zondervan, 1978), pp. 85–99.

——'Alleged errors and discrepancies in the original manuscripts of the Bible,' in Geisler (ed.), *Inerrancy*, pp. 65–7.

Bahnsen, Greg L., 'The inerrancy of the autographa', in Geisler (ed.), *Inerrancy*, pp. 149–93.

Barr, James, *The Bible in the Modern World* (London: SCM Press, 1973).

——*Fundamentalism* (London: SCM Press, 1977).

——*Holy Scripture: Canon, Authority, Criticism* (Oxford:

Clarendon Press, 1983).

Barth, Karl, *Church Dogmatics*, I/2. (Edinburgh: T&T Clark, 1956).

Barthes, Roland, *Sade / Fourier / Loyola*, trans. Richard Miller (New York: Hill and Wang, 1976).

——'The death of the author', in Roland Barthes, *Image, Music, Text*, essays selected and translated by Stephen Heath (London,: Fontana, 1977), pp. 142–8.

Barton, John, *People of the Book? The Authority of the Bible in Christianity* (London: SPCK, 1988).

Barton Payne, J., 'Higher criticism and biblical inerrancy', in Geisler (ed.), *Inerrancy*, pp. 83–113.

Beumer, Johannes, *Die katholische Inspirationslehre zwischen Vatikanum I und II: Kirchliche Dokumente im Licht der theologischen Diskussion* (Stuttgart: Katholisches Bibelwerk, 1967).

Blanchot, Maurice, *The Space of Literature*, trans. Ann Smock (Lincoln, NE: University of Nebraska Press, 1982).

Blum, Edwin A., 'The Apostles' view of Scripture', in Geisler (ed.), *Inerrancy*, pp. 37–53.

Boice, James M. (ed.) *The Foundation of Biblical Authority* (Grand Rapids: Zondervan, 1978).

Brown, Raymond E., Fitzmyer, Joseph A. and Murphy, Roland E. (eds), *The Jerome Biblical Commentary*, 2 vols (London: Geoffrey Chapman, 1968).

Bruce, F. F., *The Canon of Scripture* (Glasgow: Chapter House, 1988).

Burke, Seán, *The Death and Return of the Author: Criticism and Subjectivity in Barthes, Foucault and Derrida* (Edinburgh: Edinburgh University Press, 2nd edn., 1998).

Burtchaell, James Tunstead, *Catholic Theories of Biblical Inspiration since 1810: A Review and Critique* (Cambridge: Cambridge University Press, 1969).

Calvin, John, *Institutes of the Christian Religion*, trans. Henry Beveridge (London: James Clarke, 1949).

Carnell, Edward John, *The Case for Orthodox Theology* (Philadelphia: Westminster, 1959).

'Chicago Statement on Biblical Inerrancy', in Henry, *God, Revelation and Authority*, vol. 4, pp. 211–19.

Clark, Timothy, *The Theory of Inspiration: Composition as a crisis of subjectivity in Romantic and post-Romantic writing* (Manchester: Manchester University Press, 1997).

Clines, David J. A., *What Does Eve Do to Help? and Other Readerly Questions to the Old Testament* (*Journal for the Study of the Old Testament* Supplement Series 94) (Sheffield: Sheffield Academic Press, 1990).

Cunliffe-Jones, H., *The Authority of the Biblical Revelation* (London: James Clarke & Co., 1945).

De George, Richard T., *The Nature and Limits of Authority* (Lawrence, KS: Kansas University Press, 1985).

Derrida, Jacques, 'Che cos'è la poesia?', in Peggy Kamuf (ed.), *A Derrida Reader: Between the Blinds* (London: Harvester Wheatsheaf, 1991), pp. 221–37.

Dulles, Avery, *The Survival of Dogma* (Garden City, NY: Doubleday, 1971).

Farley, Edward, *Ecclesial Reflection* (Philadelphia: Fortress, 1982).

Farrer, Austin, *The Glass of Vision* (Westminster: Dacre Press, 1948).

Feinberg, Paul D., 'The meaning of inerrancy', in Geisler (ed.), *Inerrancy*, pp. 265–304.

Forrester, Duncan B., 'Practical Theology', in Paul Avis (ed.), *The Threshold of Theology* (Basingstoke: Marshall Pickering, 1988), 125–139.

Foucault, Michel, *The Order of Things. An Archaeology of the Human Sciences* (London: Tavistock, 1970).

Fowl, Stephen E., *Engaging Scripture* (Oxford: Blackwell,

1998).

Gaussen, L., *The Divine Inspiration of the Bible*, trans. David D. Scott (Grand Rapids: Kregel, 1971).

Geisler, Norman (ed.), *Inerrancy* (Grand Rapids: 1979).

——'The philosophical presuppositions of biblical errancy,' in Geisler (ed.), *Inerrancy*, pp. 305–34.

Gerstner, John H., 'The Church's doctrine of biblical inspiration', in James Montgomery Boice (ed.), *The Foundation of Biblical Authority* (Grand Rapids: Zondervan, 1978), pp. 23–58.

——'The view of the bible held by the Church: Calvin and the Westminster Divines', in Geisler (ed.), *Inerrancy*, pp. 383–410.

——'A Protestant view of biblical authority', in Greenspahn (ed.), *Scripture in the Jewish and Christian Traditions: Authority, Interpretation, Relevance*, pp. 41–63.

Gnuse, Robert, *The Authority of the Bible: Theories of Inspiration, Revelation, and the Canon of Scripture* (New York/Mahwah: Paulist Press, 1985).

Goldingay, John, *Models for Scripture* (Grand Rapids: Eerdmans, 1994).

Gore, Charles, 'The Holy Spirit and inspiration', in Charles Gore (ed.), *Lux Mundi: A Series of Studies in the Religion of the Incarnation* (London: John Murray, 1890), pp. 313–62.

Greenspahn, Frederick (ed.), *Scripture in the Jewish and Christian Traditions: Authority, Interpretation, Relevance* (Nashville: Abingdon, 1982).

Grillmeier, Alois, in H. Vorgrimler (ed.), *Commentary on the Documents of Vatican II*, 5 vols (London: Burns & Oates, 1967–9), vol. 3, pp. 199–246.

Hanson, R. P. C., *The Attractiveness of God* (London: SPCK, 1973).

Härle, Wilfried, *Dogmatik* (Berlin: de Gruyter, 1995).

Hauschild, Wolf-Dieter, *Lehrbuch der Kirchen- und Dog-*

mengeschichte, 2 vols, (Gütersloh: Chr. Kaiser/Gütersloh Verlagshaus, 1999–2000).

Heidegger, Martin, *Being and Time*, trans. John Macquarrie and Edward Robinson (Oxford: Blackwell, 1962).

Henry, Carl F. H., *God, Revelation and Authority*, 6 vols (Waco, TX: Word Books, 1976–83).

——'The view of the Bible held by the Church: The Early Church through Luther,' in Geisler (ed.), *Inerrancy*, pp. 355–82.

Hirsch, Emanuel (ed.), *Hilfsbuch zum Studium der Dogmatik: Die Dogmatik der Reformatoren und der altevangelischen Lehrer quellenmäßig belegt und verdeutlicht* (Berlin and Leipzig: Walter de Gruyter, 1937, 1951).

Hodge, Archibald Alexander, *Evangelical Theology* (Edinburgh: Banner of Truth Trust, 1976).

——and Warfield, Benjamin Breckenridge, Inspiration', *The Presbyterian Review* 7 (April 1881), 225–60.

Hodge, Charles, *Systematic Theology*, 3 vols (New York: Scribner's, 1899; reprinted London: James Clarke, 1960).

Ince, W. R., *The Poetic Theory of Paul Valéry: Inspiration and Technique* (Leicester: Leicester University Press, 1961).

Jaspers, Karl, *Von der Wahrheit* (Munich: Piper, 1947).

——*Way to Wisdom: An Introduction to Philosophy*, trans. Ralph Manheim (London: Victor Gollancz, 1951).

——*Der philosophische Glaube angesichts der Offenbarung* (Munich: Piper, 1962).

——*Philosophy is for Everyman: A Short Course in Philosophical Thinking*, trans. R. F. C. Hull and Grete Wels (London: Hutchinson, 1967).

——*Philosophical Faith and Revelation*, trans. E. B. Ashton (London: Collins, 1967).

——*Philosophy*, 3 vols, trans. E. B. Ashton (Chicago: University of Chicago Press, 1969–1971).

——*Chiffren der Transzendenz* (Munich: Piper, 1970).

——and Bultmann, Rudolf, *Myth and Christianity*, trans. Norbert Guterman (New York: Noonday Press, 1958).

Jeanrond, Werner, 'After hermeneutics: The relationship between theology and biblical studies', in Francis Watson (ed.), *The Open Text* (London: SCM Press, 1993), pp. 85–101.

Jüngel, Eberhard; Krodel, Gerhard; Marlé, René; and Zizioulas, John D., 'Four preliminary considerations on the concept of authority', *Ecumenical Review* xxi (1969), pp. 150–2.

Kant, Immanuel, 'An answer to the question: "What is Enlightenment"', in *Kant: Political Writings*, trans. H. B. Nisbet, ed. Hans Reiss (Cambridge: Cambridge University Press, 1991), pp. 54–60.

Kelly, J. N. D., *A Commentary on the Pastoral Epistles* (London: Adam & Charles Black, 1963).

Kelsey, David H., *The Uses of Scripture in Recent Theology* (London: SCM Press, 1975).

Kierkegaard, Søren, *Concept of Anxiety*, ed. and trans. with introduction and notes by Reidar Thomte in collaboration with Albert B. Anderson (Princeton, NJ: Princeton University Press, 1980).

——Søren Kierkegaard's Journals and Papers, ed. and trans. Howard V. Hong and Edna H. Hong, 7 vols (Bloomington, IN: Indiana University Press, 1967–78).

——*Sickness unto Death*, ed. and trans. Howard V. Hong and Edna H. Hong (Princeton, NJ: Princeton University Press, 1980).

——*Philosophical Fragments / Johannes Climacus*, ed. and trans. Howard V. Hong and Edna H. Hong (Princeton, NJ: Princeton University Press, 1985).

——*Practice in Christianity*, ed. and trans. Howard V. Hong and Edna H. Hong (Princeton, NJ: Princeton University Press, 1991).

——*Concluding Unscientific Postscript to Philosophical*

Fragments, ed. and trans. Howard V. Hong and Edna H. Hong, 2 vols (Princeton, NJ: Princeton University Press, 1992).

Körtner, Ulrich H. J., *Der inspirierte Leser: Zentrale Aspekte biblischer Hermeneutik* (Göttingen: Vandenhoeck & Ruprecht, 1994).

Kümmel, W. G., *Introduction to the New Testament* (London: SCM Press, 1975).

Lash, Nicholas, *Voices of Authority* (London: Sheed and Ward, 1976).

Law, David R., *Kierkegaard as Negative Theologian* (Oxford: Clarendon Press, 1993).

Leech, Kenneth, *Spirituality and Pastoral Care* (London: Sheldon, 1986).

Lindsell, Harold, *The Battle for the Bible* (Grand Rapids: Zondervan, 1976).

Lonergan, Bernard J. F., *A Second Collection*, ed. William F. J. Ryan and Bernard J. Tyrell (London: Darton, Longman & Todd, 1974).

Lovelace, Richard, 'Inerrancy: Some historical perspectives', in Nicole and Ramsey Michaels (eds), *Inerrancy and Common Sense*, pp. 15–47.

Lüdemann, Gerd, *Das Unheilige in der heiligen Schrift: Die andere Seite der Bibel* (Stuttgart: Radius, 1996).

Luther, Martin, *D. Martin Luthers Werke*, 64 vols (Weimar: Hermann Böhlau and successor, 1883–1990).

Macquarrie, John, *Existentialism* (Harmondsworth: Penguin, 1973).

——*Principles of Christian Theology* (London: SCM Press, 1977).

Marcel, Pierre Ch., 'Our Lord's use of Scripture', in Henry (ed.), *Revelation and the Bible*, pp. 119–34.

M'Caig, A., *The Grand Old Book, being Lectures on Inspiration and Higher Criticism* (London: Elliot Stock, 1894).

McKim, Donald K. (ed.), *The Authoritative Word. Essays on the Nature of Scripture* (Grand Rapids: Eerdmans, 1983).

Montgomery, John Warwick (ed.), *God's Inerrant Word: An International Symposium on the Trustworthiness of Scripture* (Minneapolis: Bethany, 1974).

Murray, John 'The attestation of Scripture', in Westminster Seminary, *The Infallible Word: A Symposium*, pp. 1–54.

Nicole, Roger R. 'The Nature of Inerrancy,' in Nicole and Ramsey Michaels (eds), *Inerrancy and Common Sense*, pp. 71–95.

——'New Testament use of the Old Testament', in Henry (ed.), *Revelation and the Bible*, pp. 135–51.

——and Ramsey Michaels, J. (eds), *Inerrancy and Common Sense* (Grand Rapids, Michigan: Baker Book House, 1980).

O'Collins, Gerald, SJ, *Fundamental Theology* (London: Darton, Longman & Todd, 1981).

Olson, Alan M., *Transcendence and Hermeneutics: An Interpretation of the Philosophy of Karl Jaspers* (The Hague: Martinus Nijhoff, 1979).

Pache, René, *The Inspiration and Authority of Scripture*, trans. Helen I. Needham (Chicago: Moody Press, 1969).

Packer, James, *'Fundamentalism' and the Word of God* (London: Inter-Varsity Press, 1958).

Pannenberg, Wolfhart, 'The crisis of the scripture principle,' in *Basic Questions in Theology*, trans. George H. Kehm, 3 vols (London: SCM Press, 1970–73), vol. 1, pp. 1–14.

Pinnock, Clark H., *Biblical Revelation – The Foundation of Christian Theology* (Chicago: Moody Press, 1971).

——A Defense of Biblical Infallibility (Philadelphia: Presbyterian and Reformed Publishing Co., 1967).

——'The inspiration of Scripture and the authority of Jesus Christ', in Montgomery (ed.), *God's Inerrant Word,* pp. 201–18.

Pius XII, *Encyclical Letter: Divino Afflante Spiritu*, trans. G. D. Smith (London: Catholic Truth Society, 1944).

Preus, Jacob A. O., *It is Written* (St Louis: Concordia, 1971).

Preus, Robert, *The Inspiration of Scripture: A Study of the Theology of the Seventeenth Century Lutheran Dogmaticians* (Edinburgh: Oliver and Boyd, 1957).

Rahner, Karl, *Inspiration in the Bible* (New York: Herder and Herder, 1961).

Reid, J. K. S., *The Authority of Scripture: A Study of the Reformation and Post-Reformation Understanding of the Bible* (London: Methuen, 1957).

Reventlow, Henning Graf, *The Authority of the Bible and the Rise of the Modern World*, trans. John Bowden (London: SCM Press, 1984).

Ricoeur, Paul, 'The hermeneutics of symbols and philosophical reflection: I', in Paul Ricoeur, *The Conflict of Interpretations: Essays in Hermeneutics*, ed. Don Ihde (Evanston: Northwestern University Press, 1974), pp. 287–314.

Rogers, Jack B., 'The church doctrine of biblical authority', in McKim (ed.), *The Authoritative Word*, pp. 197–224.

Sabatier, Auguste, *The Religions of Authority and the Religions of the Spirit* (London: Williams & Norgate, 1904).

Sanday, William, *Inspiration* (London: Longmans, Green & Co, 1896).

Sagan, Carl, *The Demon-Haunted World. Science as a Candle in the Dark* (London: Headline, 1997).

Sartre, Jean-Paul, *Being and Nothingness: An Essay on Phenomenological Ontology*, trans. Hazel E. Barnes (New York: Philosophical Library, no date).

Schleiermacher, Friedrich, *The Christian Faith*, ed. H. R. Mackintosh and J. S. Stewart (Edinburgh: T&T Clark, 1989).

Schroeder, H. J. (ed.), *Canons and Decrees of the Council of*

Trent (St Louis, MO: B. Herder, 1941).

Schweizer, Eduard, *θεοπνευστος*, in Gerhard Kittel (ed.), *Theological Dictionary of the New Testament*, trans. and ed. Geoffrey W. Bromiley, 10 vols (Grand Rapids: Eerdmans, 1964–76).

Schwöbel, Christoph, 'Kirche als Communio', in Wilfried Härle and Reiner Preul, *Marburger Jahrbuch Theologie, VIII: Kirche* (Marburg: N. G. Elwert, 1996), pp. 11–46.

Semmelroth, Otto and Zerwick, Maximilian, *Vatikanum II über das Wort Gottes* (Stuttgart: Katholisches Bibelwerk, 1966).

Smith, Richard J. 'Inspiration and inerrancy', in Brown, Fitzmyer and Murphy, *Jerome Biblical Commentary*, vol. 2, pp. 499–514.

Sproul, Robert, 'The case for inerrancy: A methodological analysis,' in Montgomery (ed.), *God's Inerrant Word*, pp. 242–61.

Stibbs, Alan M., 'The witness of Scripture to its inspiration', in Henry (ed.), *Revelation and the Bible*, pp. 105–18.

Stuart, Douglas, 'Inerrancy and textual criticism,' in Nicole and Ramsey Michaels, *Inerrancy and Common Sense*, pp. 97–117.

Stuhlmacher, P., *Vom Verstehen des Neuen Testaments: Eine Hermeneutik* (Göttingen; Vandenhoeck & Ruprecht, 1979).

Tigerstedt, E. N., *Plato's Idea of Poetical Inspiration* (Helsinki-Helsingfors: Commentationes Humanarum Litterarum, Societas Scientiarum Fennica, 1969).

Tillich, Paul, *Systematic Theology* (London: SCM Press, 1951).

Tomes, Roger, 'Do we need a doctrine of inspiration?', *Theology Themes*, vol. 3, no. 2 (Spring 1995), pp. 18–22.

Vawter, Bruce, *Biblical Inspiration* (London: Hutchinson, 1972).

von Campenhausen, Hans, *The Formation of the Christian Bible* (London: Adam & Charles Black, 1972).

Wand, J. W. C., *The Authority of the Scriptures* (London: A. R. Mowbray, 1949).

Warfield, Benjamin Breckinridge, *The Inspiration and Authority of the Bible*, ed. Samuel Craig (Philadelphia: Presbyterian and Reformed Publishing Company, 1970).

——*Limited Inspiration* (Philadelphia: Presbyterian and Reformed Publishing Company, no date).

——'The inerrancy of the original autographs', in *Selected Shorter Writings of Benjamin B. Warfield*, ed. John E. Meeter (Nutley, NJ: Presbyterian and Reformed Publishing Company, 1973), vol. 2.

——and Hodge, Archibald Alexander, 'Inspiration', *The Presbyterian Review* 7 (April 1881), pp. 225–60.

Watson, Francis, *Text and Truth* (Edinburgh: T&T Clark, 1997).

Wenham, John, *Christ and the Bible* (London: Tyndale, 1972).

——'Christ's view of Scripture', in Geisler (ed.), *Inerrancy*, pp. 3–36.

Wesley, John, *Journal*, in Nehemiah Curock (ed.), *The Journal of the Rev. John Wesley, A. M.*, 8 vols (London: Robert Culley (vol 1), Charles H. Kelly (vols 2–8), pp. 1909–16).

Westminster Seminary, *The Infallible Word: A Symposium* (Phillipsburg, NJ: Presbyterian and Reformed Publishing Co., 1978).

Wood, Charles M., *The Formation of Christian Understanding: An Essay in Theological Hermeneutics* (Philadelphia: Westminster, 1981).

World Council of Churches, *Faith and Order: Louvain 1971. Study Reports and Documents* (Faith and Order Paper 59; Geneva, 1971).

Young, Edward J., *Thy Word is Truth* (Grand Rapids: Eerdmans, 1957).

——'The authority of the Old Testament', in Westminster Seminary, *Infallible Word*, pp. 55–91.

Index

BIBLE REFERENCES